Company's Coming®

Cook For Kids

Jean Paré

www.**companys**coming.com
visit our web-site

Front Cover

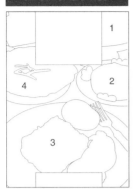

Front Cover

1. Cheesecake Bundt, page 82
2. Chewy Wheat And Fruit Salad, page 74
3. Lasagne Florentine, page 48
4. Chicken Taco Salad, page 56

Props Courtesy Of: The Bay
Wal-Mart Canada Inc.

Back Cover

Back Cover

1. Alphabet Soup, page 64
2. Lunch Bag Wraps, page 40
3. Dirt Cups, page 134

Props Courtesy Of: The Bay

Second Printing July 2001

Canadian Cataloguing in Publication Data

Paré, Jean
Company's Coming, cook for kids
Includes index.
ISBN 1-895455-65-0

1. Cookery. 2. Children—Nutrition

TX652.5.C66 2001   641.5'622   C00-901545-0

Published in Canada by
COMPANY'S COMING PUBLISHING LIMITED
2311 - 96 Street
Edmonton, Alberta, Canada T6N 1G3
Tel: (780) 450-6223   Fax: (780) 450-1857
www.companyscoming.com

Company's Coming is a registered trademark owned by
Company's Coming Publishing Limited
Printed in Canada

Cooking Tonight?
Drop by companyscoming.com

companyscoming.com

Who We Are | Browse Cookbooks | Cooking Tonight? | Home

everyday ingredients

feature recipes

feature recipes —— Cooking tonight? Check out this month's *feature recipes*—absolutely FREE!

tips and tricks —— Looking for some great kitchen helpers? *tips and tricks* is here to save the day!

reader circle —— In search of answers to cooking or household questions? Do you have answers you'd like to share? Join the fun with *reader circle*, our on-line question and answer bulletin board. Our *reader circle chat room* connects you with cooks from around the world. Great for swapping recipes too!

cooking links —— Other interesting and informative web-sites are just a click away with *cooking links.*

experts on-line —— Consult *experts on-line* for Jean Paré's time-saving tips and advice.

keyword search —— Find cookbooks by title, description or food category using *keyword search*.

e-mail us —— We want to hear from you—*e-mail us* lets you offer suggestions for upcoming titles, or share your favorite recipes.

Company's Coming
COOKBOOKS®

everyday
recipes trusted
by millions

Company's Coming Cookbooks

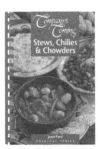

Original Series

- 150 Delicious Squares*
- Casseroles*
- Muffins & More*
- Salads*
- Appetizers
- Desserts
- Soups & Sandwiches
- Cookies*
- Vegetables
- Main Courses
- Pasta*
- Cakes
- Barbecues*
- Pies*
- Light Recipes*
- Preserves*
- Light Casseroles*
- Chicken*
- Kids Cooking
- Breads*
- Meatless Cooking*
- Cooking For Two*
- Breakfasts & Brunches*
- Slow Cooker Recipes*
- Pizza*
- One Dish Meals*
- Starters*
- Stir-Fry*
- Make-Ahead Meals*
- The Potato Book*
- Low-Fat Cooking*
- Low-Fat Pasta*
- Appliance Cooking*
- Cook For Kids
- Stews, Chilies & Chow
- **NEW** Oct 1/01

Greatest Hits Series

- Biscuits, Muffins & Loaves
- Dips, Spreads & Dressings
- Soups & Salads
- Sandwiches & Wraps
- Italian
- Mexican

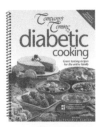

Lifestyle Series

- Grilling
- Diabetic Cooking

Special Occasion Series

- Chocolate Everything
- Gifts from the Kitchen **NEW** Sept 1/01

Table of Contents

The Company's Coming Story

Jean Paré grew up understanding that the combination of family, friends and home cooking is the essence of a good life. From her mother she learned to appreciate good cooking, while her father praised even her earliest attempts. When she left home she took with her many acquired family recipes, a love of cooking and an intriguing desire to read recipe books like novels!

"never share a recipe you wouldn't use yourself"

In 1963, when her four children had all reached school age, Jean volunteered to cater the 50th anniversary of the Vermilion School of Agriculture, now Lakeland College. Working out of her home, Jean prepared a dinner for over 1000 people which launched a flourishing catering operation that continued for over eighteen years. During that time she was provided with countless opportunities to test new ideas with immediate feedback—resulting in empty plates and contented customers! Whether preparing cocktail sandwiches for a house party or serving a hot meal for 1500 people, Jean Paré earned a reputation for good food, courteous service and reasonable prices.

"Why don't you write a cookbook?" Time and again, as requests for her recipes mounted, Jean was asked that question. Jean's response was to team up with her son, Grant Lovig, in the fall of 1980 to form Company's Coming Publishing Limited. April 14, 1981, marked the debut of "150 DELICIOUS SQUARES", the first Company's Coming cookbook in what soon would become Canada's most popular cookbook series.

Jean Paré's operation has grown steadily from the early days of working out of a spare bedroom in her home. Full-time staff includes marketing personnel located in major cities across Canada. Home Office is based in Edmonton, Alberta in a modern building constructed specially for the company.

Today the company distributes throughout Canada and the United States in addition to numerous overseas markets, all under the guidance of Jean's daughter, Gail Lovig. Best-sellers many times over in English, Company's Coming cookbooks have also been published in French and Spanish. Familiar and trusted in home kitchens around the world, Company's Coming cookbooks are offered in a variety of formats, including the original softcover series.

Jean Paré's approach to cooking has always called for quick and easy recipes using everyday ingredients. Even when traveling, she is constantly on the lookout for new ideas to share with her readers. At home, she can usually be found researching and writing recipes, or working in the company's test kitchen. Jean continues to gain new supporters by adhering to what she calls "the golden rule of cooking": never share a recipe you wouldn't use yourself. It's an approach that works—*millions of times over!*

Foreword

Cooking food for children that they will eat and like can by enjoyable and rewarding! After all, there are so many things to applaud in a child's life, even if you only look at the traditional reasons such as birthdays, graduations and holidays. Whatever the occasion, you will find the perfect recipe combinations within these pages. Cook For Kids is organized according to when the food might be eaten, such as breakfast, lunch, supper and snack time. Each of the 16 photographs has a kid's occasion theme that will help you develop a menu that is sure to please.

It isn't just the special occasions that we find ourselves cooking for kids, it's each and every day. And getting kids to eat has its challenges, we know! The recipes in this cookbook are straightforward, using common ingredients and they answer the question of what to make for dinner. Have your children look through Cook For Kids to pick out some recipes they'd like you to make and they'll be more tempted to try them. When putting together any meal, remember the four food groups and prepare the food in such a way that they have more nutritive value. This means baking potatoes rather than frying them, waiting to add salt until you've tasted the dish or choosing lean ground beef over regular. Exposing children to a variety of foods can bring about a surprised, "Hey, this is good!" Presentation can also make a big difference in how food is received. Dressing up your table with bright colors may be just the ticket to getting your kids' appetites rarin' to go.

Whether it's spring break, video night, a bag lunch or dinner tonight, Cook For Kids has it covered with over 135 kid-friendly recipes.

Jean Paré

Each recipe has been analyzed using the most updated version of the Canadian Nutrient File from Health Canada which is based upon the United States Department of Agriculture (USDA) Nutrient Data Base.

Margaret Ng, B.Sc. (Hon), M.A.
Registered Dietitian

Granola

Send in a small, resealable plastic bag as a snack for recess, or mix with yogurt for a quick lunch. Delicious with milk for breakfast. Can be stored at room temperature in sealed container for up to 2 weeks or chilled for up to 3 weeks.

Large flake rolled oats (old-fashioned)	4 cups	1 L
Corn flakes cereal	3 cups	750 mL
Flake coconut	1/2 cup	125 mL
Skim milk powder	1/2 cup	125 mL
Dark raisins	1/3 cup	75 mL
Finely diced dried apricots	1/3 cup	75 mL
Roasted shelled sunflower seeds	1/4 cup	60 mL
Sesame seeds	2 tbsp.	30 mL
Cooking oil	1/4 cup	60 mL
Unsweetened apple juice	1/2 cup	125 mL
Liquid honey	2 tbsp.	30 mL

Combine first 8 ingredients in large roaster.

Drizzle cooking oil over top while tossing.

Combine apple juice and honey in small bowl. Drizzle half over cereal mixture while tossing. Bake, uncovered, in 275°F (140°C) oven for 15 minutes. Stir. Drizzle with remaining juice mixture. Stir. Bake for 15 minutes. Stir. Bake for 30 minutes until golden. Makes 7 3/4 cups (1.9 L).

1/2 cup (125 mL): 223 Calories; 8.9 g Total Fat; 82 mg Sodium; 7 g Protein; 31 g Carbohydrate; 3 g Dietary Fiber

Grape Jelly Oats

If your child won't eat plain oatmeal,
try this disguised version. Serve with milk.

Water	2 2/3 cups	650 mL
Grape jelly	1/2 cup	125 mL
Salt	1/4 tsp.	1 mL
Dried blueberries (or raisins)	1/2 cup	125 mL
Quick-cooking rolled oats (not instant or large flake)	1 1/3 cups	325 mL

Bring water, jelly, salt and blueberries to a boil in medium saucepan. Stir in rolled oats. Heat, uncovered, on low for 4 minutes, stirring occasionally, until soft and thickened. Makes 3 cups (750 mL).

3/4 cup (175 mL): 261 Calories; 2.1 g Total Fat; 184 mg Sodium; 5 g Protein; 58 g Carbohydrate; 5 g Dietary Fiber

Microwave Directions For 1 Serving: Microwave 2/3 cup (150 mL) water, 2 tbsp. (30 mL) jelly, sprinkle of salt and 2 tbsp. (30 mL) blueberries in microwave-safe cereal bowl on high (100%) for 1 minute. Stir in 1/3 cup (75 mL) rolled oats. Microwave on low (30%) for 1 1/2 to 2 minutes until soft and thickened. Makes about 1 cup (250 mL).

Paré Pointer
Getting a personal fowl is having your own chicken.

Double-Decker French Toast

This french toast does double duty—for breakfast or for lunch.

Spreadable cream cheese	2 tbsp.	30 mL
White (or whole wheat) bread slices	4	4
Jam (or jelly)	4 tsp.	20 mL
Large eggs	2	2
Milk	1 tbsp.	15 mL
Granulated sugar	1 tsp.	5 mL
Vanilla	1/2 tsp.	2 mL
Salt	1/8 tsp.	0.5 mL

Divide and spread cream cheese on 1 side of 2 bread slices up to edge. Divide and spread jam on cream cheese, keeping 1/2 to 3/4 inch (12 to 20 mm) away from edge. Cover with remaining slices of bread. Press lightly around edges to seal.

Beat remaining 5 ingredients together with fork in pie plate. Spray non-stick frying pan with no-stick cooking spray. Heat until hot. Holding sandwich together, dip both sides into egg mixture. Place in frying pan. Repeat with remaining sandwich. Slowly pour any remaining egg mixture onto bread. Cook on medium until golden. Turn over. Cook until golden and firm. Cut in half diagonally. Makes 4 triangles.

1 triangle: 164 Calories; 6 g Total Fat; 283 mg Sodium; 6 g Protein; 21 g Carbohydrate; 1 g Dietary Fiber

APPLE CINNAMON TOAST: Omit jam. Divide and spread 3 tbsp. (50 mL) finely diced apple on 1 side of 2 bread slices. Mix 1/8 tsp. (0.5 mL) cinnamon and 1/2 tsp. (2 mL) brown sugar in small cup. Sprinkle over apples. Cover with remaining slices of bread. Press lightly around edges to seal. Proceed as above.

SALSA 'N' CHEESE TOAST: Omit jam. Divide and spread 2 tsp. (10 mL) chunky salsa on 1 side of 2 bread slices. Divide and sprinkle 2 tbsp. (30 mL) grated Cheddar cheese over salsa. Cover with remaining slices of bread. Press lightly around edges to seal. Omit sugar and vanilla in egg mixture. Proceed as above.

(continued on next page)

MEXI-TOAST: Omit jam. Divide and sprinkle 2 tbsp. (30 mL) grated Cheddar cheese, 2 tsp. (10 mL) chopped green onion and 2 tsp. (10 mL) chopped red pepper on 1 side of 2 bread slices. Cover with remaining slices of bread. Press lightly around edges to seal. Omit sugar and vanilla in egg mixture. Proceed as above.

Take-Along Breakfast Bars

For those who roll out of bed and run out the door!

Quick-cooking rolled oats (not instant)	4 cups	1 L
Medium unsweetened coconut	2 cups	500 mL
Lightly crushed corn flakes cereal	1 cup	250 mL
Chopped dried apricots	1 cup	250 mL
Raisins	1 cup	250 mL
Shelled roasted sunflower seeds	2/3 cup	150 mL
Hard margarine (or butter)	1/2 cup	125 mL
Can of sweetened condensed milk	11 oz.	300 mL
Corn syrup	1/4 cup	60 mL
Frozen concentrated orange juice	2 tbsp.	30 mL

Combine first 6 ingredients in large bowl.

Melt margarine in medium saucepan. Add remaining 3 ingredients. Heat and stir on low until combined. Pour over granola mixture while tossing. Mixture will be quite sticky. Pack firmly into 2 greased 9 x 13 inch (22 x 33 cm) pans. Bake in 325°F (160°C) oven for 20 to 30 minutes until edges are golden. Score while warm. Let cool on wire rack. Cut into 2 x 3 inch (5 x 7.5 cm) bars. Wrap individual bars in plastic wrap. Makes 30 bars.

1 bar: 216 Calories; 10.8 g Total Fat; 71 mg Sodium; 4 g Protein; 28 g Carbohydrate; 2 g Dietary Fiber

TAKE-ALONG BREAKFAST COOKIES: Roll out mixture between greased waxed paper to 1/2 inch (12 mm) thick. Cut into shapes with cookie cutter. Transfer carefully to greased cookie sheet. Bake in 325°F (160°C) oven for 15 to 20 minutes until edges are golden. Let cool on wire rack. Wrap individual cookies in plastic wrap. Makes about 24 cookies.

Pictured on page 18.

Cinnamon Cheese Pancakes

Delicious with maple syrup or strawberries.

All-purpose flour	1 1/4 cups	300 mL
Baking powder	1 tsp.	5 mL
Granulated sugar	2 tbsp.	30 mL
Ground cinnamon	1/2 tsp.	2 mL
Salt	1/2 tsp.	2 mL
Large eggs, fork-beaten	4	4
Creamed cottage cheese	1 cup	250 mL
Plain yogurt	1 cup	250 mL
Cooking oil	1/2 tsp.	2 mL

Combine first 5 ingredients in medium bowl. Make a well in center.

Combine eggs, cottage cheese and yogurt in small bowl. Add to well. Stir until just moistened.

Heat cooking oil in non-stick frying pan on medium-high. Pour 1/4 cup (60 mL) batter for each pancake. Cook, uncovered, for 3 minutes per side until golden brown. Keep warm in oven until all batter is used. Makes 12 pancakes.

1 pancake: 114 Calories; 2.6 g Total Fat; 234 mg Sodium; 7 g Protein; 15 g Carbohydrate; trace Dietary Fiber

Lemon Cheese

Excellent spread on toast or muffins.

Butter (not margarine)	1/4 cup	60 mL
Granulated sugar	1 cup	250 mL
Freshly squeezed lemon juice (about 1 medium)	1/3 cup	75 mL
Grated lemon peel	1 1/2 tsp.	7 mL
Large eggs, fork-beaten	3	3
Drops of yellow food coloring (optional)	2	2

(continued on next page)

Breakfast

Melt butter in medium saucepan. Stir in sugar until dissolved.

Stir in lemon juice, lemon peel and eggs. Heat and stir on medium until starting to boil and thicken. Remove from heat. Stir in food coloring. Cool completely. Store in refrigerator. Makes 3 1/3 cups (825 mL).

2 tbsp. (30 mL): 54 Calories; 2.3 g Total Fat; 25 mg Sodium; 1 g Protein; 8 g Carbohydrate; trace Dietary Fiber

Happy Face Pancakes

Pancakes with a chocolate smile—what a terrific way to start the day.

All-purpose flour	1 cup	250 mL
Granulated sugar	2 tsp.	10 mL
Baking powder	2 tsp.	10 mL
Salt	1/2 tsp.	2 mL
Large egg	1	1
Mashed ripe banana (about 1 small)	1/3 cup	75 mL
Cooking oil	2 tbsp.	30 mL
Milk	3/4 cup	175 mL
Chocolate chips (or blueberries)	70 - 80	70 - 80

Stir first 4 ingredients in medium bowl. Make a well in center.

Beat next 4 ingredients in small bowl. Add to well. Stir until just moistened.

Pour 1/4 cup (60 mL) into non-stick frying pan for each pancake. Cook for about 30 seconds. Arrange chocolate chips on pancakes in happy face shape. Turn pancakes over when edges start to dry and bubbles break on surface. Cook until golden. Makes 8 pancakes.

1 pancake: 148 Calories; 6.2 g Total Fat; 195 mg Sodium; 4 g Protein; 20 g Carbohydrate; 1 g Dietary Fiber

Pictured on page 17.

Breakfast Oatmeal Cookies

Milk and cookies for breakfast!

Hard margarine (or butter), softened	2/3 cup	150 mL
Brown sugar, packed	3/4 cup	175 mL
Frozen concentrated orange juice	2 tbsp.	30 mL
Vanilla	2 tsp.	10 mL
Large eggs, fork-beaten	2	2
Unsweetened applesauce	1/2 cup	125 mL
Whole wheat flour	1 cup	250 mL
Baking powder	1 tsp.	5 mL
Baking soda	1 tsp.	5 mL
Salt	1 tsp.	5 mL
Flake coconut	1 1/2 cups	375 mL
Quick-cooking rolled oats (not instant)	2 1/2 cups	625 mL
Chopped dried mixed fruit (apricots, blueberries, cranberries, cherries, dates)	2 cups	500 mL

Cream margarine and brown sugar together in large bowl. Stir in orange juice, vanilla and eggs until well combined. Stir in applesauce.

Combine flour, baking powder, baking soda and salt in small bowl. Add to applesauce mixture. Stir well.

Gradually stir in coconut, rolled oats and mixed fruit until well combined. Drop by tablespoonfuls onto greased cookie sheet. Bake on center rack in 350°F (175°C) oven for 16 minutes until golden and firm. Makes 60 cookies.

1 cookie: 84 Calories; 4.2 g Total Fat; 98 mg Sodium; 1 g Protein; 11 g Carbohydrate; 1 g Dietary Fiber

Breakfast-In-A-Baggie

Hand this to your children as they run out the door.
Can be stored in resealable freezer bags in the freezer.

Chopped dried apricots	3/4 cup	175 mL
Chopped dried apples (or pineapple)	3/4 cup	175 mL
Dried cranberries	3/4 cup	175 mL
Almonds, with skin	1 cup	250 mL
Rice squares cereal	1 1/2 cups	375 mL
Diced whole wheat (or multi-grain) bagels (about 2 medium)	3 cups	750 mL
Canola oil	1/4 cup	60 mL
Brown sugar, packed	1 tbsp.	15 mL
Ground cinnamon	1/2 tsp.	2 mL
Vanilla	1 tsp.	5 mL
Salt	1/4 tsp.	1 mL

Combine first 6 ingredients in large bowl.

Combine next 4 ingredients in liquid measure cup. Drizzle over cereal mixture while tossing. Spread out on large baking sheet. Bake in 250°F (120°C) oven for 45 minutes to 1 hour, stirring every 15 minutes, until toasted and bagel is dried.

Sprinkle with salt. Cool completely. Makes 8 cups (2 L).

1 cup (250 mL): 323 Calories; 17.6 g Total Fat; 208 mg Sodium; 6 g Protein; 40 g Carbohydrate; 6 g Dietary Fiber

 Buy dried fruit in small quantities for freshness and optimum taste. They can become overly dry and hard when stored for long periods.

Apple Stack

This is the best breakfast because it can be eaten with your fingers!

Liquid honey	1 tbsp.	15 mL
Whole wheat flour tortillas	2	2
(8 inch, 20 cm, size)		
Ground cinnamon	1/4 tsp.	1 mL
Grated Cheddar (or Monterey Jack	1 cup	250 mL
or mozzarella) cheese,		
or combination of all 3		
Very thinly sliced apple	1 cup	250 mL
(about 1 small)		

Divide and spread honey on 1 side of each tortilla. Divide and sprinkle cinnamon over honey. Place 1 tortilla, honey side up, on ungreased baking sheet. Divide and sprinkle 1/2 of cheese over cinnamon on 1 tortilla, keeping 1/2 inch (12 mm) from edge. Arrange apples evenly on cheese. Cover with remaining 1/2 of cheese. Place remaining tortilla on top, honey side down. Press down slightly. Bake in 400°F (205°C) oven for about 8 minutes until edges are crisp and cheese is melted. Let cool slightly. Cuts into 4 wedges.

1 wedge: 204 Calories; 10.5 g Total Fat; 297 mg Sodium; 9 g Protein; 20 g Carbohydrate; 2 g Dietary Fiber

Breakfast

1. Fritter Muffins, page 21
2. Raisin Buttermilk Biscuits, page 23
3. Banana Yogurt Shake, page 147
4. Happy Face Pancakes, page 13

Props Courtesy Of: Le Gnome
Winners Stores

Oatmeal Blueberry Muffins

Oatmeal goodness in a fruity muffin.

Quick-cooking rolled oats (not instant)	1 cup	250 mL
1% buttermilk (or sour milk)	1 cup	250 mL
Dried blueberries	3/4 cup	175 mL
All-purpose flour	1 cup	250 mL
Brown sugar, packed	3/4 cup	175 mL
Baking powder	1 tsp.	5 mL
Baking soda	1/2 tsp.	2 mL
Salt	1/2 tsp.	2 mL
Large egg, fork-beaten	1	1
Hard margarine (or butter), melted	1/4 cup	60 mL

Combine first 3 ingredients in medium bowl. Let stand for 15 minutes.

Combine next 5 ingredients in large bowl. Make a well in center.

Add egg and margarine to rolled oats mixture. Stir. Add to well. Stir until just moistened. Fill each greased muffin cup with about 1/4 cup (60 mL) batter. Bake in 400°F (205°C) oven for about 15 minutes until wooden pick inserted in center of muffin comes out clean. Let stand for 5 minutes before removing to rack to cool. Makes 12 muffins.

1 muffin: 192 Calories; 5.1 g Total Fat; 251 mg Sodium; 4 g Protein; 34 g Carbohydrate; 2 g Dietary Fiber

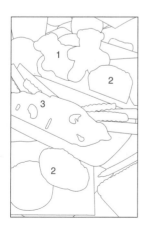

Bag Lunch

1. Take-Along Breakfast Cookies, page 11
2. Fruit And Fiber Muffins, page 22
3. CLT Pita Pockets, page 42

Props Courtesy Of: Elephants Never Forget Etc.
Winners Stores

Apple Crunch Muffins

Crunchy on the top, moist in the center.

TOPPING

Brown sugar, packed	2 tbsp.	30 mL
Quick-cooking rolled oats (not instant)	2 tbsp.	30 mL
All-purpose flour	1 tbsp.	15 mL
Ground cinnamon	1/8 tsp.	0.5 mL
Hard margarine (or butter)	1 tbsp.	15 mL
All-purpose flour	1 cup	250 mL
Whole wheat flour	2/3 cup	150 mL
Brown sugar, packed	1/3 cup	75 mL
Baking powder	4 tsp.	20 mL
Salt	1/2 tsp.	2 mL
Ground cinnamon	1/2 tsp.	2 mL
Large egg	1	1
Milk	1 cup	250 mL
Cooking oil	1/4 cup	60 mL
Vanilla	1 tsp.	5 mL
Peeled and finely chopped apple	1 cup	250 mL

Topping: Combine first 4 ingredients in small bowl. Cut in margarine until crumbly. Set aside.

Stir both flours, brown sugar, baking powder, salt and cinnamon in large bowl. Make a well in center.

Beat next 4 ingredients in medium bowl. Stir in apple. Add to well. Stir until just moistened. Fill greased muffin cups 3/4 full. Sprinkle with topping. Bake in 400°F (205°C) oven for about 15 minutes until wooden pick inserted in center of muffin comes out clean. Let stand for 5 minutes before removing to rack to cool. Makes 12 muffins.

1 muffin: 178 Calories; 6.8 g Total Fat; 149 mg Sodium; 4 g Protein; 26 g Carbohydrate; 2 g Dietary Fiber

Fritter Muffins

A traditional treat with a bacon twist.
Serve with jam or ketchup.

Yellow cornmeal	1 cup	250 mL
1% buttermilk (or sour milk)	1 cup	250 mL
Large egg, fork-beaten	1	1
Cooking oil	1/4 cup	60 mL
Can of cream-style corn	14 oz.	398 mL
Bacon slices, cooked crisp and crumbled (or 1/3 cup, 75 mL, imitation bacon bits)	6	6
All-purpose flour	1 cup	250 mL
Brown sugar, packed	2 tbsp.	30 mL
Baking powder	4 tsp.	20 mL
Baking soda	1/2 tsp.	2 mL
Salt	1/2 tsp.	2 mL

Stir cornmeal and buttermilk in medium bowl. Let stand for 10 minutes.

Stir in next 4 ingredients.

Stir remaining 5 ingredients in large bowl. Make a well in center. Add cornmeal mixture to well. Stir until just moistened. Fill greased muffin cups 3/4 full. Bake in 425°F (220°C) oven for about 15 minutes until wooden pick inserted in center of muffin comes out clean. Let stand for 5 minutes before removing to rack to cool. Makes 12 muffins.

1 muffin: 197 Calories; 7.5 g Total Fat; 358 mg Sodium; 5 g Protein; 28 g Carbohydrate; 1 g Dietary Fiber

Pictured on page 17.

Paré Pointer

Sure this coffee tastes like mud. It was ground five minutes ago.

Fruit And Fiber Muffins

A mouthful of goodness in every bite.

All-purpose flour	1 cup	250 mL
Whole wheat flour	1/4 cup	60 mL
Oat bran	1/4 cup	60 mL
Ground cinnamon	2 tsp.	10 mL
Baking soda	1 1/2 tsp.	7 mL
Baking powder	1 1/2 tsp.	7 mL
Salt	1/2 tsp.	2 mL
Grated carrot	1 cup	250 mL
Finely chopped apple, with peel	2 cups	500 mL
Raisins	1/2 cup	125 mL
Chopped pecans (optional)	1/2 cup	125 mL
Large eggs, fork-beaten	2	2
Milk	1 1/4 cups	300 mL
Cooking oil	1/4 cup	60 mL
Vanilla	1 tsp.	5 mL
Unsweetened applesauce (or mashed banana)	1/3 cup	75 mL
Liquid honey	1/4 cup	60 mL

Combine first 7 ingredients in large bowl.

Stir in carrot, apple, raisins and pecans. Make a well in center.

Beat next 4 ingredients together in small bowl. Pour into well. Stir.

Add applesauce and honey. Stir until just moistened. Fill each greased muffin cup 3/4 full. Bake in 375°F (190°C) oven for 20 minutes until wooden pick inserted in center of muffin comes out clean. Let stand for 5 minutes before removing to rack to cool. Makes about 12 muffins.

1 muffin: 187 Calories; 6.4 g Total Fat; 315 mg Sodium; 4 g Protein; 30 g Carbohydrate; 2 g Dietary Fiber

Pictured on page 18.

Raisin Buttermilk Biscuits

Best when served warm with honey or butter.

All-purpose flour	1 1/2 cups	375 mL
Whole wheat flour	1/2 cup	125 mL
Brown sugar, packed	1 tbsp.	15 mL
Baking powder	1 tbsp.	15 mL
Salt	1/2 tsp.	2 mL
Baking soda	1/2 tsp.	2 mL
Ground cinnamon	1/2 tsp.	2 mL
Dark raisins	1/2 cup	125 mL
Hard margarine (or butter), melted	1/4 cup	60 mL
1% buttermilk	3/4 cup	175 mL

Combine first 8 ingredients in large bowl. Make a well in center.

Add margarine and buttermilk to well. Stir gently with fork until dough starts to form a ball. Turn out onto lightly floured surface. Knead gently 8 to 10 times. Pat out to 3/4 inch (2 cm) thickness. Cut 2 inch (5 cm) circles, or other shapes, with floured cutter. Place on ungreased baking sheet. Bake in 425°F (220°C) oven for 12 to 15 minutes until golden. Makes about 12 biscuits.

1 biscuit: 143 Calories; 4.2 g Total Fat; 237 mg Sodium; 3 g Protein; 24 g Carbohydrate; 1 g Dietary Fiber

Pictured on page 17.

Variation: Omit raisins. Add same amount of dried cranberries, blueberries or currants.

 If you don't usually have fresh buttermilk on hand, buy powdered buttermilk. To reconstitute, use 3 tbsp. (50 mL) powder plus water for each 1 cup (250 mL) buttermilk required.

Chicken Puffed Pockets

Why buy the commercial stuffed pockets when they are so easy to make?

Frozen bread dough, thawed	1 lb.	454 g
FILLING		
Chopped cooked chicken (or turkey or ham)	1 cup	250 mL
Salad dressing (or mayonnaise)	2 tbsp.	30 mL
Grated sharp Cheddar cheese	1/2 cup	125 mL
Grated mozzarella cheese	1/2 cup	125 mL
Finely sliced green onion (optional)	1	1
No-salt seasoning (such as Mrs. Dash)	1/4 tsp.	1 mL
Seasoned salt	1/4 tsp.	1 mL
Pepper, sprinkle		
Hard margarine (or butter), melted	1 tbsp.	15 mL
Grated Parmesan cheese (or sesame seeds), sprinkle		

Cut dough into 8 portions. Roll each portion out to 6 inch (15 cm) circle on lightly floured surface.

Filling: Combine first 8 ingredients in medium bowl. Makes 1 2/3 cups (400 mL) filling. Place 3 tbsp. (50 mL) filling on each circle of dough. Dampen edges with water. Fold dough over top of filling. Pinch closed. Seal with tip of fork. Place on greased baking sheet.

Brush tops with margarine. Sprinkle with Parmesan cheese. Bake in 350°F (175°C) oven for 18 to 22 minutes until golden. Makes 8 pockets.

1 pocket: 274 Calories; 12 g Total Fat; 442 mg Sodium; 14 g Protein; 27 g Carbohydrate; 1 g Dietary Fiber

Mozza Subs

These can be assembled ahead and baked when needed for a quick tasty lunch.

Hard margarine (or butter), softened	4 tsp.	20 mL
Small submarine buns, split	4	4
Pizza sauce	6 tbsp.	100 mL
Thinly sliced red onion (optional)	3/4 cup	175 mL
Thinly sliced yellow pepper (optional)	3/4 cup	175 mL
Sliced mozzarella cheese (not process)	8 oz.	225 g
Thinly sliced pepperoni sausage	4 oz.	113 g
Thinly sliced salami sausage	4 oz.	113 g
Sliced mozzarella cheese (not process)	8 oz.	225 g

Divide and spread margarine on each bun half. Lay, cut side up, on baking sheet. Spread with pizza sauce.

Layer remaining 6 ingredients, in order given, on sauce. Bake in 350°F (175°C) oven for 15 to 20 minutes until bun is crisp and cheese is melted. Makes 4 subs.

1 sub: 848 Calories; 52.3 g Total Fat; 1985 mg Sodium; 42 g Protein; 51 g Carbohydrate; 2 g Dietary Fiber

Paré Pointer
If a farmer's hogs went on strike, they would form "pigget" lines.

Meatball Heroes

Mild in flavor, strong in appeal. Serve with corn chips, carrot and celery sticks.

Lean ground beef	1 lb.	454 g
Fine dry bread crumbs	3/4 cup	175 mL
Garlic clove, minced	1	1
Small onion	1/2	1/2
Large egg	1	1
Milk	1/3 cup	75 mL
Grated light Parmesan cheese	1/3 cup	75 mL
Salt	1/2 tsp.	2 mL
Parsley flakes	1/2 tsp.	2 mL
Dried whole oregano	1/4 tsp.	1 mL
Pepper	1/8 tsp.	0.5 mL
Cooking oil	2 tsp.	10 mL
Small onion, thinly sliced rings	1	1
Small green pepper, chopped	1	1
Spaghetti sauce	2 cups	500 mL
Water	1/4 cup	60 mL
Small submarine buns, split	7 - 8	7 - 8

Combine ground beef and bread crumbs in large bowl.

Process next 9 ingredients in blender or food processor until smooth. Add to beef mixture. Stir well. Form into 1/2 inch (12 mm) balls. Place on lightly greased baking sheet. Bake in 425°F (220°C) oven for 10 minutes until no pink remains in beef. Remove to paper towel to drain.

Heat cooking oil in large frying pan. Sauté onion for about 2 minutes until soft. Add green pepper. Sauté for about 3 minutes until soft. Stir in spaghetti sauce and water. Add meatballs. Cover. Simmer for 20 minutes, stirring occasionally.

Remove small amount of bread from inside of each bun half. Toast, cut side up, under broiler. Fill bottom halves with meatballs and sauce. Cover with top halves. Makes 7 to 8 subs.

1 sub: 462 Calories; 11.9 g Total Fat; 1284 mg Sodium; 25 g Protein; 63 g Carbohydrate; 3 g Dietary Fiber

Pictured on page 108.

Snappy Fish Dog

A crispy, golden filling makes this a very different but a very good dog.

Frozen fish sticks	2	2
Light salad dressing (or mayonnaise)	1 tbsp.	15 mL
Parsley flakes	1/8 tsp.	0.5 mL
Sweet pickle relish	1 tsp.	5 mL
Hot dog bun, split	1	1

Arrange fish sticks on ungreased baking sheet. Bake in 450°F (230°C) oven for 10 to 12 minutes, turning over at half-time.

Stir salad dressing, parsley and relish together in small bowl.

Spread salad dressing mixture on bun. Arrange fish sticks on top. Makes 1 fish dog.

1 fish dog: 332 Calories; 13.1 g Total Fat; 687 mg Sodium; 12 g Protein; 40 g Carbohydrate; 1 g Dietary Fiber

Variation: Ketchup may be used instead of, or as well as, salad dressing mixture.

Paré Pointer
If you combine a karate expert with a pig, would you have a pork chop?

Drumsticks

So handy to have frozen for reheating in microwave. Children won't be reluctant to eat chicken with the bone in when little drumsticks just fit into little hands. Great with Honey Yogurt Dip, page 128.

Chicken drumettes	20	20
Large eggs, fork-beaten	2	2
Light sour cream	1/4 cup	60 mL
Seasoned salt	1/2 tsp.	2 mL
Pepper	1/8 tsp.	0.5 mL
Finely crushed corn flakes cereal	1/3 cup	75 mL

Cut skin and meat of drumettes around narrower end with sharp knife. Using thumb and fingers, push skin and meat to top of bone making "knob" of chicken.

Combine eggs, sour cream, seasoned salt and pepper in small cup.

Place cereal in small bowl. Dip meaty ends of drumettes into egg mixture, then into cereal. Arrange on greased baking sheet in single layer. Bake in 425°F (220°C) oven for 15 minutes. Turn over. Bake for 10 to 15 minutes until golden and juices run clear. Makes 20 drumsticks.

1 drumstick: 56 Calories; 2.7 g Total Fat; 79 mg Sodium; 6 g Protein; 2 g Carbohydrate; trace Dietary Fiber

Pictured on page 71.

To Freeze And Reheat: Arrange baked drumsticks on baking sheet. Freeze until hard. Store in resealable freezer bag in freezer. Remove desired amount. Microwave 3 drumsticks on high (100%) for 1 1/2 minutes. Or wrap in foil and warm in 250°F (120°C) for 10 minutes until heated through.

Paré Pointer
Fast-food lovers are drawn to marathons. They like to eat and run.

Plain Good Chicken Fingers

Even better dipped in Honey Yogurt Dip, page 128,
or Cranberry Dip, page 128.

Boneless, skinless chicken breast halves (about 1 lb., 454 g)	4	4
All-purpose flour	1/2 cup	125 mL
Seasoned salt	1 tsp.	5 mL
Pepper	1/4 tsp.	1 mL
Large egg, fork-beaten	1	1
Milk	1/4 cup	60 mL
Fine dry bread crumbs	2/3 cup	150 mL
Cooking oil	1 tbsp.	15 mL

Cut chicken breasts lengthwise into 1/2 inch (12 mm) strips.

Combine flour, seasoned salt and pepper on sheet of waxed paper. Coat chicken.

Combine egg and milk in glass pie plate. Place bread crumbs in shallow dish. Dip chicken into egg mixture, then into bread crumbs. Arrange on greased baking sheet in single layer. Chill for 1 hour.

Drizzle cooking oil over chicken. Bake in 350°F (175°C) oven for 30 minutes, turning over at half-time, until no pink remains. Makes about 20 chicken fingers.

1 chicken finger: 69 Calories; 1.5 g Total Fat; 118 mg Sodium; 8 g Protein; 6 g Carbohydrate; trace Dietary Fiber

Paré Pointer

Of course a cheerleader's favorite food is root beer.

Fish Fingers

Do fish have fingers?

Package of frozen cod fillets	14 1/2 oz.	400 g
Large egg, fork-beaten	1	1
Seasoned salt	1/2 tsp.	2 mL
Parsley flakes	1/2 tsp.	2 mL
Crushed plain potato chips	1 1/2 cups	375 mL

Cut fillets lengthwise, for a total of 8 pieces.

Combine egg, seasoned salt and parsley in shallow dish.

Place crushed potato chips on plate. Dip fish into egg mixture, then roll in chips. Place on greased baking sheet in single layer. Bake in 450°F (230°C) oven for 12 minutes, turning over at half-time, until golden. Do not overcook. Makes 8 fish fingers.

1 fish finger: 116 Calories; 5.3 g Total Fat; 185 mg Sodium; 10 g Protein; 6 g Carbohydrate; trace Dietary Fiber

H' Egg And Cheese Sandwich

Comfort food.

Square deli ham slice	1	1
Large egg	1	1
Salt, sprinkle		
Pepper, sprinkle		
Hard margarine (or butter), softened (optional)	2 tsp.	10 mL
Whole wheat bread slices	2	2
Process cheese slice	1	1

Fry 1 side of ham slice in non-stick frying pan on medium until golden. Turn over. Break egg onto ham. Poke yolk. Sprinkle with salt and pepper. Cook for 4 minutes. Turn over. Fry for about 1 minute until desired doneness.

(continued on next page)

Spread margarine on 1 side of both bread slices. Place ham and egg on 1 slice. Place cheese on top. Cover with second slice of bread, buttered side down. Makes 1 sandwich.

1 sandwich: 391 Calories; 20 g Total Fat; 1273 mg Sodium; 24 g Protein; 30 g Carbohydrate; 3 g Dietary Fiber

Chip 'N' Chicken Strips

Crispy and light golden in color.
Serve with Honey Yogurt Dip, page 128, or Cranberry Dip, page 128.

Large egg	1	1
Milk	1/4 cup	60 mL
Onion powder	1/2 tsp.	2 mL
Garlic powder	1/4 tsp.	1 mL
Paprika	1/2 tsp.	2 mL
Lemon juice	2 tsp.	10 mL
Coarsely crushed plain potato chips (4 3/4 oz., 130 g, bag)	2 cups	500 mL
Parsley flakes	1 tsp.	5 mL
Boneless, skinless chicken breast halves (about 4)	1 lb.	454 g

Combine first 6 ingredients in medium bowl. Beat with fork.

Combine crushed potato chips and parsley in separate medium bowl.

Cut chicken breasts lengthwise into 1/2 inch (12 mm) strips. Dip into egg mixture, then roll in chip mixture. Place on greased baking sheet in single layer. Bake in 425°F (220°C) oven for about 15 minutes until no pink remains. Makes 20 chicken strips.

1 chicken strip: 72 Calories; 2.9 g Total Fat; 58 mg Sodium; 7 g Protein; 3 g Carbohydrate; trace Dietary Fiber

Pictured on page 89.

Cheese Pinwheels

Good hot or cold. The variations below are worth a try.

Package of refrigerator crescent-style rolls (8 rolls per tube)	8 1/2 oz.	235 g
Grated sharp Cheddar cheese	1 1/3 cups	325 mL
FILLING		
Finely diced dill pickles, blotted dry	1/4 cup	60 mL
Crushed corn flakes cereal 1/2 cup	125 mL	
Crisp rice cereal	1/2 cup	125 mL

Unroll dough. Separate and shape into 4 rectangles. Pinch diagonal perforations to seal. Divide and sprinkle cheese over each.

Filling: Divide filling on rectangles. Roll up from narrow end, jelly-roll style. Pinch edge to seal.

Spread corn flake cereal on sheet of waxed paper. Spread rice cereal on second sheet. Coat 2 rolls with corn flakes cereal. Coat remaining 2 rolls with rice cereal. Cut rolls crosswise into 5 slices. Place, cut side down, on greased baking sheet. Bake in 375°F (190°C) oven for 15 to 20 minutes until golden. Makes 20 pinwheels.

1 pinwheel: 70 Calories; 4.1 g Total Fat; 139 mg Sodium; 3 g Protein; 5 g Carbohydrate; trace Dietary Fiber

Pictured on page 108.

Variation: Omit dill pickles. Use same amount of chopped nuts, finely diced peeled apple or finely chopped cooked chicken or ham.

HAM PINWHEELS: Omit Cheddar cheese and filling. Divide 1 1/3 cups (325 mL) Swiss cheese and 1/4 cup (60 mL) finely diced ham on rectangles.

MUSHROOM PINWHEELS: Omit Cheddar cheese and filling. Divide 1 1/3 cups (325 mL) mozzarella cheese and 1/4 cup (60 mL) mushrooms on rectangles.

Pizza Buns

It's quick, it's tasty—and it's pizza!

Diced pepperoni sticks	3/4 cup	175 mL
Favorite Salsa, page 130 (or commercial)	1/3 cup	75 mL
Grated part-skim mozzarella cheese	3/4 cup	175 mL
Grated Parmesan cheese	1 tbsp.	15 mL
Dried whole oregano	1/4 tsp.	1 mL
Refrigerator country-style biscuits (10 biscuits per tube)	12 oz.	340 g
Large egg, fork-beaten	1	1
Paprika, sprinkle		

Combine pepperoni, salsa, both cheeses and oregano in small bowl.

Separate biscuits. Roll or press out each on lightly floured surface to 4 inch (10 cm) circle. Place 1 1/2 tbsp. (25 mL) pepperoni mixture in center of each. Dampen edges with water. Fold dough over filling. Pinch edges closed. Place, seam side down, on greased baking sheet.

Brush tops with egg. Sprinkle with paprika. Bake in 375°F (190°C) oven for about 15 minutes until golden. Makes 10 pizza buns.

1 pizza bun: 189 Calories; 9.3 g Total Fat; 716 mg Sodium; 8 g Protein; 18 g Carbohydrate; trace Dietary Fiber

 If a loaf of bread seems dry, wrap it in a damp tea towel and chill overnight. Still wrapped, heat in 250°F (120°C) oven for 10 minutes.

Lunchtime Mac And Cheese

A microwave recipe that's just right for lunch.

Finely chopped onion	1/4 cup	60 mL
Cooking oil	1 tbsp.	15 mL
All-purpose flour	2 tbsp.	30 mL
Vegetable cocktail juice (such as V8)	2 cups	500 mL
Hot water	3/4 cup	175 mL
Elbow macaroni, uncooked	1 1/2 cups	375 mL
Grated light sharp Cheddar cheese	1 cup	250 mL

Microwave onion in cooking oil in small microwave-safe bowl on high (100%) for 2 minutes.

Sprinkle with flour. Stir. Slowly add juice and hot water. Stir in macaroni. Cover. Microwave on medium (50%) for 15 minutes.

Stir in cheese. Cover. Let stand for 5 minutes. Makes 4 cups (1 L).

1 cup (250 mL): 318 Calories; 10.3 g Total Fat; 661 mg Sodium; 14 g Protein; 41 g Carbohydrate; 2 g Dietary Fiber

Variation: Add 6 bacon slices, cooked crisp and crumbled, 1/16 tsp. (0.5 mL) each dried sweet basil and dried whole oregano and add a sprinkle of garlic powder.

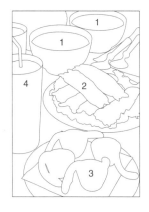

Lunch

1. Alphabet Soup, page 64
2. Lunch Bag Wraps, page 40
3. Dirt Cups, page 134
4. Melon Shake, page 149

Props Courtesy Of: The Bay

Plain Pizza

A quick lunch packed with kid-loving flavor.

Process cheese spread	2/3 cup	150 mL
Ketchup	2 tbsp.	30 mL
Whole wheat flour tortillas	2	2
(10 inch, 25 cm, size)		
Bacon slices, cooked crisp and	6	6
crumbled (or 1/3 cup, 75 mL,		
imitation bacon bits)		

Divide and spread cheese spread and ketchup on 1 side of each tortilla. Sprinkle with bacon. Place on greased baking sheet. Bake in 400°F (205°C) oven for about 10 minutes until hot. Makes 2 pizzas.

1/2 pizza: 256 Calories; 14.9 g Total Fat; 1118 mg Sodium; 13 g Protein; 19 g Carbohydrate; 2 g Dietary Fiber

Variation: Omit bacon. Add same amount of finely diced pepperoni, chopped peppers, well drained pineapple or chopped tomatoes.

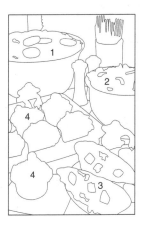

Picnic

1. Picnic Salad, page 68
2. Taco Snack Mix, page 109
3. Cheddar And Apple Pita Pockets, page 43
4. Raspberry Cupcakes, page 103

Props Courtesy Of: Dansk Gifts

Tuna Pizza

A knife and fork pizza.

CRUST

Whole wheat flour	1 1/4 cups	300 mL
All-purpose flour	3/4 cup	175 mL
Baking powder	1 tbsp.	15 mL
Salt	1 tsp.	5 mL
Instant yeast	1 tsp.	5 mL
Granulated sugar	1 tsp.	5 mL
Olive oil	1/4 cup	60 mL
Milk	1 cup	250 mL
Olive oil	2 tsp.	10 mL

TOPPING

Large roma (plum) tomatoes, sliced 1/4 inch (6 mm) thick	4	4
Dried sweet basil, crushed	1 tsp.	5 mL
Salt	1/2 tsp.	2 mL
Garlic powder (optional)	1/16 tsp.	0.5 mL
Grated part-skim mozzarella cheese	1 cup	250 mL
Can of flaked white tuna, drained	6 oz.	170 g
Grated carrot	1/2 cup	125 mL
Thinly sliced celery	1/2 cup	125 mL
Light salad dressing (or mayonnaise)	1/3 cup	75 mL
Grated light sharp Cheddar cheese	2 cups	500 mL

Crust: Combine first 6 ingredients in large bowl.

Heat first amount of olive oil and milk in small saucepan until very warm. Add to flour mixture, stirring with fork, until mixture forms a ball. Cover. Let rest for 20 minutes. Roll out and press into well greased 12 inch (30 cm) pizza pan.

Brush with second amount of olive oil.

(continued on next page)

Topping: Arrange tomato slices evenly on crust.

Combine basil, salt and garlic powder in small dish. Sprinkle over tomato.

Layer mozzarella cheese, tuna, carrot and celery on top of tomato.

Drizzle salad dressing over celery. Sprinkle with Cheddar cheese. Bake, uncovered, in 400°F (205°C) oven for 35 minutes until crust is browned and cheese is melted. Cuts into 8 to 10 wedges.

1 wedge: 405 Calories; 20.9 g Total Fat; 940 mg Sodium; 21 g Protein; 35 g Carbohydrate; 4 g Dietary Fiber

Pictured on page 144.

Tuna-Stuffed Celery

Creamy and crunchy—the perfect combination.

Celery ribs, cleaned and blotted dry	3	3
Spreadable cream cheese	2 tbsp.	30 mL
Chunk light tuna in water, drained	6 oz.	170 g
Salad dressing (or mayonnaise)	3 tbsp.	50 mL
Finely diced dill pickles	2 tbsp.	30 mL
Salt	1/8 tsp.	0.5 mL
Pepper, sprinkle		
Paprika, sprinkle		

Cut celery ribs into 2 1/2 to 3 inch (6.4 to 7.5 cm) lengths.

Combine next 6 ingredients in small bowl. Makes 3/4 cup (175 mL) filling. Spread and pack about 1/2 to 1 tbsp. (7 to 15 mL) into each celery piece.

Sprinkle with paprika. Makes 16 stuffed celery pieces.

1 stuffed celery piece: 33 Calories; 2.1 g Total Fat; 85 mg Sodium; 3 g Protein; 1 g Carbohydrate; trace Dietary Fiber

Pickle And Cheese Wraps

These store well overnight in the refrigerator.

Process cheese spread	2 tbsp.	30 mL
Whole wheat flour tortilla (8 inch, 20 cm, size)	1	1
Grated medium Cheddar cheese	2 tbsp.	30 mL
Baby dill pickles	2	2

Spread cheese spread on 1 side of tortilla. Sprinkle with Cheddar cheese. Place pickles, end to end, across bottom third of tortilla. Bring up bottom edge over pickles and roll tightly to enclose. Wrap in plastic wrap. Chill. Makes 1 wrap.

1 wrap: 269 Calories; 12.8 g Total Fat; 2082 mg Sodium; 13 g Protein; 28 g Carbohydrate; 4 g Dietary Fiber

Lunch Bag Wraps

Pack these into a small sealed container with a frozen juice pack and your children will be the envy of their lunch mates.

Very thin slices of deli ham (or roast beef or chicken), about 1/3 lb. (150 g)	6	6
Salad dressing (or mayonnaise), optional	2 tbsp.	30 mL
Prepared mustard (optional)	2 tbsp.	30 mL
Small carrot sticks	6	6
Red pepper slivers	6	6
Baby dills, quartered lengthwise	2	2
Light sharp Cheddar cheese sticks	6	6

Spread 1 side of each ham slice with salad dressing and mustard. Divide and layer remaining 4 ingredients across 1 end of ham slices. Roll up, jelly-roll style. Makes 6 wraps.

1 wrap: 152 Calories; 9.3 g Total Fat; 750 mg Sodium; 13 g Protein; 3 g Carbohydrate; trace Dietary Fiber

Pictured on page 35 and back cover.

Cheese-Stuffed Eggs

Also a great appetizer.

Large eggs	6	6
Water		
Light salad dressing (or mayonnaise)	1/4 cup	60 mL
Prepared mustard	1/2 tsp.	2 mL
Salt	1/4 tsp.	1 mL
Onion powder	1/8 tsp.	0.5 mL
Finely grated light sharp Cheddar cheese, room temperature	1/4 cup	60 mL
Process cheese spread	1 tbsp.	15 mL

Poke tiny hole in large end of each egg. Place in single layer in saucepan. Cover eggs with water to 1 inch (2.5 cm) over top. Bring to a boil. Boil slowly, uncovered, for 10 minutes. Drain. Run cold water over eggs to cool as quickly as possible. Remove shells. Cut eggs lengthwise in half. Remove yolks to small bowl.

Add next 6 ingredients to yolks. Mash well with fork. Spoon or pipe yolk mixture into cavity in egg white. Makes 12 stuffed eggs.

1 stuffed egg: 64 Calories; 4.6 g Total Fat; 169 mg Sodium; 4 g Protein; 1 g Carbohydrate; trace Dietary Fiber

Pictured on page 53.

Paré Pointer
Astronauts look forward to being down and out.

CLT Pita Pockets

Cheese, lettuce and tomato tucked into pitas. For smaller hands, try the variation below.

Diced part-skim mozzarella (or feta) cheese	1 cup	250 mL
Halved grape (or cherry) tomatoes	2 cups	500 mL
Green onions, chopped	3	3
Non-fat Italian dressing	1/4 cup	60 mL
Pita breads (6 inch, 15 cm, size), cut in half	4	4
Romaine lettuce leaves	8	8

Combine cheese, tomato, green onion and dressing in small bowl. Toss until well coated. Makes 4 cups (1 L).

Line each pita pocket with lettuce. Add 1/2 cup (125 mL) tomato mixture to each. Makes 8 stuffed pita pockets.

1 stuffed pita pocket: 144 Calories; 3.6 g Total Fat; 286 mg Sodium; 8 g Protein; 20 g Carbohydrate; 1 g Dietary Fiber

Pictured on page 18.

Variation: Use smaller 3 inch (7.5 cm) size pita breads slit open at top. Line with lettuce. Add 1/4 cup (60 mL) filling to each. Makes 16 pita pockets.

Apple Sandwiches

The sprouts give a pleasant crunch in this sandwich.

Apple, peeled and cored	1	1
Lemon juice	2 tsp.	10 mL
Spreadable cream cheese	1/3 cup	75 mL
Liquid honey	1 tbsp.	15 mL
Ground cinnamon, sprinkle		
Raisin (or whole wheat) bread slices	4	4
Alfalfa sprouts (optional)	1/2 cup	125 mL

(continued on next page)

Thinly slice apple. Toss with lemon juice in small bowl.

Combine cream cheese, honey and cinnamon in separate small bowl. Divide and spread on 1 side of each bread slice. Drain apples. Blot dry. Arrange on 2 bread slices.

Top with sprouts. Cover with remaining 2 bread slices. Makes 2 sandwiches.

1 sandwich: 343 Calories; 15.8 g Total Fat; 303 mg Sodium; 7 g Protein; 47 g Carbohydrate; 3 g Dietary Fiber

Cheddar And Apple Pita Pockets

Most kids will love this combination.

Diced mild Cheddar cheese	3/4 cup	175 mL
Diced red apple, with peel	1 cup	250 mL
Diced celery	1/2 cup	125 mL
Salad dressing (or mayonnaise)	3 tbsp.	50 mL
Plain yogurt	3 tbsp.	50 mL
Brown sugar, packed	1 1/2 tbsp.	25 mL
Ground cinnamon	1/4 tsp.	1 mL
Pita breads (6 inch, 15 cm, size), cut in half	2	2
Romaine lettuce leaves	4	4

Combine cheese, apple and celery in medium bowl.

Stir salad dressing, yogurt, brown sugar and cinnamon together in small bowl. Add to apple mixture. Stir well.

Line each pita pocket with lettuce. Fill each with 1/2 cup (125 mL) apple mixture. Makes 4 stuffed pita pockets.

1 stuffed pita pocket: 300 Calories; 15.5 g Total Fat; 365 mg Sodium; 11 g Protein; 30 g Carbohydrate; 1 g Dietary Fiber

Pictured on page 36.

Stacked Chili Wedges

A different way to serve chili. Add a salad for a complete meal.

Lean ground beef	3/4 lb.	340 g
Chopped onion	1/4 cup	60 mL
Chopped celery	1/4 cup	60 mL
Chopped green pepper	1/4 cup	60 mL
Chili powder	2 tsp.	10 mL
Garlic salt	1/2 tsp.	2 mL
Granulated sugar	1/4 tsp.	1 mL
Hot pepper sauce	1/4 tsp.	1 mL
Can of crushed tomatoes	14 oz.	398 mL
Can of red kidney beans, drained, rinsed and mashed	14 oz.	398 mL
Grated light Monterey Jack cheese	1 cup	250 mL
Chili-flavored flour (or whole wheat) tortillas (8 inch, 20 cm, size)	6	6
Grated light Monterey Jack cheese	1 cup	250 mL

Scramble-fry ground beef, onion, celery and green pepper in non-stick frying pan until vegetables are soft and no pink remains in beef. Drain.

Stir in chili powder, garlic salt, sugar and pepper sauce. Stir in tomatoes, kidney beans and first amount of cheese until well combined. Makes 4 cups (1 L) filling.

Press 1 tortilla into greased 9 inch (22 cm) springform pan to fit. Spread with 3/4 cup (175 mL) chili mixture. Repeat with remaining tortillas and chili, ending with tortilla on top. Sprinkle with second amount of cheese. Cover with greased foil. Bake in 350°F (175°C) oven for about 1 1/4 hours until hot in center. Remove foil. Broil until cheese is browned. Let stand for 15 minutes before cutting. Remove pan sides. Cuts into 12 wedges.

1 wedge: 227 Calories; 10.1 g Total Fat; 488 mg Sodium; 14 g Protein; 21 g Carbohydrate; 4 g Dietary Fiber

Pictured on page 72.

Supper

No Beans! Chili

Lots of kids will be happy to have chili without beans!

Lean ground beef	1 lb.	454 g
Chopped onion	1/2 cup	125 mL
Chopped celery	1/2 cup	125 mL
Water	3 cups	750 mL
Can of tomato sauce	14 oz.	398 mL
Can of stewed tomatoes, with juice, mashed	14 oz.	398 mL
Chili powder	2 tsp.	10 mL
Salt	1 tsp.	5 mL
Pepper	1/4 tsp.	1 mL
Grated carrot	3/4 cup	175 mL
Frozen peas	3/4 cup	175 mL
Frozen kernel corn	3/4 cup	175 mL
Orzo pasta (or other small pasta), uncooked	1 cup	250 mL
Grated light sharp Cheddar cheese	1 cup	250 mL

Scramble-fry ground beef, onion and celery in non-stick frying pan for about 15 minutes until vegetables are soft and no pink remains in beef. Drain. Turn into large pot or Dutch oven.

Stir in water, tomato sauce, tomatoes with juice, chili powder, salt and pepper. Bring to a boil. Stir in carrot, peas, corn and pasta. Return to a boil. Reduce heat to medium. Simmer, uncovered, stirring occasionally, for about 30 minutes until pasta is tender but firm and chili is thick.

Sprinkle cheese on individual servings. Makes 8 1/2 cups (2.1 L).

1 cup (250 mL): 304 Calories; 9.4 g Total Fat; 865 mg Sodium; 19 g Protein; 36 g Carbohydrate; 4 g Dietary Fiber

Pictured on page 89.

Saucy Meatballs

Kids love the sauce served over rice too.

Large eggs, fork-beaten	2	2
Ketchup	1/4 cup	60 mL
Soy sauce	2 tbsp.	30 mL
Seasoned salt	1 tsp.	5 mL
Onion powder	1/4 tsp.	1 mL
Garlic powder	1/4 tsp.	1 mL
Soda cracker crumbs	1 1/4 cups	300 mL
Extra lean ground beef	2 lbs.	900 g
SAUCE		
Cranberry jelly	1 cup	250 mL
Can of tomato sauce	7 1/2 oz.	213 mL
Granulated sugar	1 tbsp.	15 mL
White vinegar	1 tbsp.	15 mL
Onion powder	1/4 tsp.	1 mL
Ground cloves, just a pinch		

Combine eggs, ketchup, soy sauce, seasoned salt, onion powder and garlic powder in small bowl. Mix well. Add cracker crumbs. Stir.

Mix in ground beef. Shape into 1 1/2 inch (3.8 cm) balls. Makes about 60 meatballs. Place in 3 1/2 quart (3.5 L) slow cooker.

Sauce: Mix all 6 ingredients in medium bowl. Makes 2 3/4 cups (675 mL) sauce. Pour over meatballs. Cover. Cook on Low for 6 to 7 hours or on High for 3 to 3 1/2 hours. Serves 10.

1 serving: 342 Calories; 15.5 g Total Fat; 761 mg Sodium; 26 g Protein; 24 g Carbohydrate; trace Dietary Fiber

Pictured on page 90.

Variation: To bake in oven, combine meatballs and sauce in 3 quart (3 L) casserole. Cover. Bake in 325°F (160°C) oven for 2 hours.

Oriental Meatballs

Kids and adults alike will enjoy these meatballs
with lots of sauce, served over rice.

Lean ground beef	1 lb.	454 g
Large egg, fork-beaten	1	1
Salt	1/2 tsp.	2 mL
Pepper	1/8 tsp.	0.5 mL
Green onions, finely sliced	2	2
Light sour cream	1/2 cup	125 mL
Fine dry bread crumbs	1/3 cup	75 mL
SAUCE		
Brown sugar, packed	2/3 cup	150 mL
Cornstarch	3 tbsp.	50 mL
Dry mustard	2 tsp.	10 mL
Pineapple juice	1 cup	250 mL
White vinegar	1/2 cup	125 mL
Soy sauce	1 1/2 tsp.	7 mL
Ketchup	1/2 cup	125 mL
Water	1/2 cup	125 mL

Combine first 7 ingredients in medium bowl until well mixed. Shape into 1 inch (2.5 cm) meatballs. Arrange in single layer on greased baking sheet. Bake in 350°F (175°C) oven for 15 minutes until firm and no pink remains in beef. Remove to paper towel to drain. Makes about 70 meatballs.

Sauce: Combine brown sugar, cornstarch and mustard in large saucepan. Stir in remaining 5 ingredients. Heat and stir on medium until boiling and thickened. Makes 2 3/4 cups (675 mL) sauce. Add meatballs. Stir. Serves 8.

1 serving: 256 Calories; 7 g Total Fat; 522 mg Sodium; 13 g Protein; 36 g Carbohydrate; trace Dietary Fiber

Paré Pointer

After several poor plays, the game was lost.
That's how the rookie fumbles.

Lasagne Florentine

Get the whole family to eat spinach and
enjoy it in this delicious lasagne.

Virgin olive oil (or cooking oil)	1 tbsp.	15 mL
Extra lean ground beef	1 lb.	454 g
Garlic cloves, minced	2	2
Chopped onion	1/2 cup	125 mL
Can of tomato sauce	14 oz.	398 mL
Can of tomato paste	5 1/2 oz.	156 mL
Water	1 cup	250 mL
Brown sugar, packed	1 tsp.	5 mL
Salt	1/2 tsp.	2 mL
Dried sweet basil	1 tsp.	5 mL
Dried whole oregano	1/2 tsp.	2 mL
Lasagna noodles	9	9
Boiling water	12 cups	3 L
Salt	1 tbsp.	15 mL
Frozen chopped spinach, thawed and squeezed dry	10 oz.	300 g
Part-skim ricotta cheese	2 cups	500 mL
Large eggs, fork-beaten	2	2
Grated light Parmesan cheese	1/4 cup	60 mL
Grated part-skim mozzarella cheese	2 cups	500 mL

Heat olive oil in large frying pan. Scramble-fry ground beef, garlic and onion until onion is soft and no pink remains in beef. Drain.

Add next 7 ingredients. Stir. Simmer, uncovered, for 30 minutes until slightly reduced and thickened. Makes 4 cups (1 L) sauce.

Cook noodles in boiling water and salt in large uncovered pot or Dutch oven for 12 to 15 minutes until tender but firm. Drain. Rinse with cold water. Drain.

Combine next 4 ingredients in medium bowl.

(continued on next page)

Assemble in layers in greased 9 x 13 inch (22 x 33 cm) baking pan as follows:
1. 1 cup (250 mL) sauce
2. 3 lasagna noodles
3. 1 1/2 cups (375 mL) sauce
4. 3 lasagna noodles
5. All of spinach/cheese mixture
6. 3 lasagna noodles
7. Remaining sauce
8. All of mozzarella cheese

Cover with greased foil. Bake in 350°F (175°C) oven for 1 hour. Remove foil. Heat under broiler until cheese is browned. Let stand, uncovered, for 10 minutes before cutting. Cuts into 8 to 10 pieces.

1 piece: 428 Calories; 19.1 g Total Fat; 840 mg Sodium; 33 g Protein; 21 g Carbohydrate; 3 g Dietary Fiber

Pictured on front cover.

Beef And Macaroni

Nothing to it. Just scramble-fry the ground beef and put everything into one pot. No need to precook the pasta.

Lean ground beef	1 1/2 lbs.	680 g
Chopped onion	1 cup	250 mL
Elbow macaroni, uncooked	1 1/2 cups	375 mL
Chopped green or red pepper	1/2 cup	125 mL
Chopped celery	1/2 cup	125 mL
Can of tomato sauce	7 1/2 oz.	213 mL
Can of diced tomatoes	28 oz.	796 mL
Water	1 cup	250 mL
Worcestershire sauce	1 tsp.	5 mL
Salt	1 tsp.	5 mL
Pepper	1/4 tsp.	1 mL
Italian seasoning mix (optional)	1/2 tsp.	2 mL

Scramble-fry ground beef and onion in large frying pan until no pink remains in beef.

Add remaining 10 ingredients. Stir. Cover. Simmer for 18 to 20 minutes until pasta is tender but firm. Makes 8 cups (2 L).

1 cup (250 mL): 301 Calories; 13.5 g Total Fat; 743 mg Sodium; 20 g Protein; 25 g Carbohydrate; 3 g Dietary Fiber

Fricassee In A Bowl

*A delicious way to use up leftover turkey. Don't be intimidated
by the length of the recipe. Fricassee can be made ahead and chilled or
made while the bread bowl is baking.*

BREAD BOWLS

Water	2/3 cup	150 mL
Hard margarine (or butter)	1/4 cup	60 mL
All-purpose flour	1 cup	250 mL
Grated Parmesan cheese	1/4 cup	60 mL
Baking powder	2 tsp.	10 mL
Large eggs	4	4
Cornmeal	1 tbsp.	15 mL

FRICASSEE

Chopped onion	1/2 cup	125 mL
Sliced celery	1/2 cup	125 mL
Margarine (or butter)	2 tsp.	10 mL
Can of condensed chicken broth	10 oz.	284 mL
Parsley flakes	1 tsp.	5 mL
Dried thyme	1/4 tsp.	1 mL
Pepper	1/8 tsp.	0.5 mL
Thinly sliced carrot	1/2 cup	125 mL
Peeled and thinly sliced broccoli stems	1/2 cup	125 mL
Broccoli florets	2 cups	500 mL
Frozen peas, thawed and drained	1 cup	250 mL
Can of skim evaporated milk	13 1/2 oz.	385 mL
All-purpose flour	1/4 cup	60 mL
Sherry (or alcohol-free sherry)	1 tbsp.	15 mL
Chopped cooked turkey (or chicken)	2 cups	500 mL

Bread Bowls: Place water and margarine in medium saucepan. Bring to a
boil on medium. Add flour, cheese and baking powder. Heat and stir until
mixture forms a ball. Remove from heat. Stir in eggs, 1 at a time, until
absorbed and dough is smooth and shiny.

(continued on next page)

Supper

Grease 6 medium ramekin bowls. Coat with cornmeal. Place 1/3 cup (75 mL) dough in each. Bake in 425°F (220°C) oven for 20 minutes until golden and puffy. Cool for 5 minutes before removing to serving plate.

Fricassee: Sauté onion and celery in margarine in large saucepan until soft.

Stir in broth, parsley, thyme and pepper. Bring to a boil. Add carrot and broccoli stems. Reduce heat. Cover. Simmer for 5 minutes. Add broccoli florets and peas. Cover. Simmer for 3 minutes.

Whisk evaporated milk into flour until smooth. Stir into vegetable mixture. Heat and stir until boiling and thickened. Add sherry and turkey. Stir until heated through. Fill bread bowls with about 1 cup (250 mL) fricassee. Makes 6 filled bowls.

1 filled bowl: 451 Calories; 16.8 g Total Fat; 722 mg Sodium; 34 g Protein; 40 g Carbohydrate; 4 g Dietary Fiber

Variation: Omit making bread bowls. Grease 2 quart (2 L) round casserole or two 9 inch (22 cm) round cake pans. Coat with 1/4 cup (60 mL) cornmeal. Press dough in bottom to edge. Bake in 425°F (220°C) oven for 25 to 30 minutes until puffed and browned. Center should be firm, not doughy. Make shallow cut with point of knife in center to allow steam to escape. Cool for 5 minutes before removing to serving plate. Fill with fricassee.

Variation: Omit making bread bowls. Use 6 crusty rolls. Cut top 1/4 off each bun. Hollow out inside, leaving 1/2 inch (12 mm). Broil until crisp and browned. Fill each roll with 1/2 cup (125 mL) fricassee.

 If you need a large mixing bowl but don't have one, substitute a turkey roaster, soup pot or canning kettle.

Easy Chicken Meal

Potatoes and chicken in a creamy sauce that will appeal to most children. Serve with a salad.

Boneless, skinless chicken breast halves (about 1 1/2 lbs., 680 g)	6	6
Unpeeled medium potatoes, cubed	6	6
Chopped onion	1 cup	250 mL
Can of condensed cream of chicken soup	10 oz.	284 mL
Light sour cream	1/2 cup	125 mL
Milk	1/2 cup	125 mL
Beef bouillon powder	1 tbsp.	15 mL
Dill weed	1/2 tsp.	2 mL
Pepper	1/4 tsp.	1 mL
Paprika	1/2 tsp.	2 mL

Cut each chicken breast into 6 pieces. Place in ungreased 9 x 13 inch (22 x 33 cm) shallow baking pan. Add potato and onion. Mix.

Stir remaining 7 ingredients in medium bowl. Spoon onto chicken mixture. Spread but do not stir. Cover. Bake in 375°F (190°C) oven for 1 1/4 to 1 1/2 hours until potato is tender. Serves 6.

1 serving: 330 Calories; 6.4 g Total Fat; 800 mg Sodium; 34 g Protein; 33 g Carbohydrate; 3 g Dietary Fiber

Easter

1. Springtime Ham, page 59
2. Baby Butterfly Cupcakes, page 102
3. Egg Nests, page 141
4. Cheese-Stuffed Eggs, page 41
5. Dilled Carrots And Beans, page 69

Props Courtesy Of: The Bay

Sesame Drums

Crispy golden coating with a mild flavor.

Light mayonnaise (not salad dressing)	1/2 cup	125 mL
Onion powder	1/2 tsp.	2 mL
Garlic powder	1/2 tsp.	2 mL
Salt	1/2 tsp.	2 mL
Pepper	1/4 tsp.	1 mL
Chicken drumsticks, skin removed, blotted dry	8	8
Soda cracker crumbs	2/3 cup	150 mL
Sesame seeds, toasted	1/3 cup	75 mL

Combine first 5 ingredients in medium bowl.

Add chicken. Toss to coat.

Combine cracker crumbs and sesame seeds in resealable freezer bag. Add drumsticks, a few at a time. Toss to coat. Place in single layer on greased baking sheet. Bake in 425°F (220°C) oven for 30 minutes until no pink remains in chicken and coating is crisp and browned. Makes 8 sesame drums.

1 sesame drum: 188 Calories; 10.2 g Total Fat; 425 mg Sodium; 15 g Protein; 9 g Carbohydrate; 1 g Dietary Fiber

Graduation

1. Ice Cream Sundae Cake, page 84
2. Linguine With Saucy Ham And Peas, page 62
3. Fried Cheese Balls, page 110

Props Courtesy Of: Dansk Gifts

Chicken Taco Salad

Eat the salad out of the bowl and then eat the bowl!

Lean ground chicken	1 lb.	454 g
Garlic cloves, minced	2	2
Chopped onion	1/2 cup	125 mL
Chopped green pepper	1/2 cup	125 mL
Can of tomato sauce	7 1/2 oz.	213 mL
Salt	1 tsp.	5 mL
Chili powder	1 tsp.	5 mL
Paprika	1 tsp.	5 mL
Dried whole oregano	1/2 tsp.	2 mL
Dried crushed chilies (optional)	1/4 tsp.	1 mL
Pepper	1/4 tsp.	1 mL
Ground cumin	1/8 tsp.	0.5 mL
Cornstarch	1 tsp.	5 mL
Small taco bowls (available in deli department of grocery store)	6	6
Shredded lettuce	8 cups	2 L
Diced tomato	1 1/2 cups	375 mL
Green onions, sliced (optional)	3	3
French dressing	6 tbsp.	100 mL
Grated light sharp Cheddar cheese	1 1/2 cups	375 mL
Quartered cherry tomatoes, for garnish	12	12

Scramble-fry chicken, garlic, onion and green pepper in large non-stick frying pan until no pink remains in chicken. Drain.

Combine next 9 ingredients in small bowl. Add to chicken mixture. Stir. Simmer, uncovered, for 15 minutes until thickened.

Fill each taco bowl with 1 1/4 cups (300 mL) lettuce, 1/4 cup (60 mL) tomato and 1 tbsp. (15 mL) green onion. Drizzle with 1 tbsp. (15 mL) dressing. Spoon scant 1/2 cup (125 mL) chicken mixture onto salad. Sprinkle with cheese. Garnish with cherry tomatoes. Makes 6 taco salads in bowls.

1 salad in bowl: 331 Calories; 15.9 g Total Fat; 1184 mg Sodium; 28 g Protein; 19 g Carbohydrate; 2 g Dietary Fiber

Pictured on front cover.

Saucy Chicken Melts

Perfect open-faced sandwich for younger taste buds.

Cooking oil	1 tsp.	5 mL
Lean ground chicken	3/4 lb.	340 g
Sliced green onion	1/4 cup	60 mL
Can of tomato sauce	7 1/2 oz.	213 mL
Prepared mustard	1/2 tsp.	2 mL
Seasoned salt	1/2 tsp.	2 mL
Pepper, sprinkle		
English muffins, split	5	5
Grated part-skim mozzarella cheese	1 cup	250 mL

Heat cooking oil in frying pan. Scramble-fry chicken until browned and no longer pink.

Combine next 5 ingredients in medium bowl. Add chicken. Stir.

Spread about 3 tbsp. (50 mL) chicken mixture on each muffin half. Top each with 1 1/2 tbsp. (25 mL) cheese. Bake in 375°F (190°C) oven for 12 to 15 minutes until heated through and cheese is melted. Makes 10 melts.

1 melt: 152 Calories; 3.6 g Total Fat; 371 mg Sodium; 14 g Protein; 16 g Carbohydrate; 1 g Dietary Fiber

Pictured on page 125.

Paré Pointer

The famous writer disconnected his doorbell.
He wanted to win the no-bell prize.

Turkey Rigatoni

A delicious way to use up leftover turkey.

Rigatoni pasta (about 3 1/2 cups, 875 mL)	8 oz.	225 g
Boiling water	12 cups	3 L
Salt	1 tbsp.	15 mL
Milk	2 cups	500 mL
Can of skim evaporated milk	13 1/2 oz.	385 mL
All-purpose flour	6 tbsp.	100 mL
Salt	1/2 tsp.	2 mL
Onion powder	1/4 tsp.	1 mL
Garlic powder	1/8 tsp.	0.5 mL
Ground nutmeg	1/8 tsp.	0.5 mL
Ground thyme	1/8 tsp.	0.5 mL
Celery seed	1/8 tsp.	0.5 mL
Grated light Parmesan cheese	2/3 cup	150 mL
Grated light sharp Cheddar cheese	1 cup	250 mL
Chopped cooked turkey	2 cups	500 mL
Chopped cooked broccoli	3 cups	750 mL
Part-skim mozzarella cheese	1 cup	250 mL

Cook pasta in boiling water and salt in large uncovered pot or Dutch oven for 10 minutes. Drain. Rinse with cold water. Drain. Turn into greased 3 quart (3 L) casserole.

Heat milk in large saucepan until hot.

Stir evaporated milk and flour in small bowl until smooth. Add to milk. Stir. Add salt, onion powder, garlic powder, nutmeg, thyme and celery seed. Stir. Heat on medium-low until boiling and thickened.

Add Parmesan cheese and Cheddar cheese. Heat and stir until Cheddar cheese is melted. Gently stir in turkey and broccoli. Pour over pasta in casserole. Mix until evenly coated. Smooth top.

(continued on next page)

Supper

Sprinkle with mozzarella cheese. Bake in 325°F (160°C) oven for 30 minutes until hot and bubbly and cheese is melted. Makes 11 1/2 cups (2.9 L). Serves 8.

1 serving: 371 Calories; 9.2 g Total Fat; 621 mg Sodium; 33 g Protein; 37 g Carbohydrate; 2 g Dietary Fiber

Pictured on page 126.

Springtime Ham

There are pretty peach pinwheels on this ham.

Cooked ham	4 - 5 lbs.	1.8 - 2.3 kg
Can of peach halves, juice reserved	14 oz.	398 mL
Maraschino cherries	3	3
Liquid honey	1/4 cup	60 mL
Brown sugar, packed	1/4 cup	60 mL
Dijon mustard	1 tbsp.	15 mL

Place ham on rack in medium roaster or shallow casserole. Cut each peach half into 4 slices. Arrange 3 pinwheel designs on ham with cherry in center. Secure with wooden picks pushed in just under surface of peaches so tips don't burn.

Combine reserved peach juice, honey, brown sugar and mustard in small saucepan. Bring to a boil. Cook for about 10 minutes, stirring occasionally, until slightly reduced and thickened. Pour over ham. Bake, uncovered, in 325°F (160°C) oven for 1 1/2 hours, brushing with drippings 3 or 4 times. Add 1/4 cup (60 mL) hot water for final 30 minutes of baking if there are no drippings. Pour drippings over ham before serving. Serves 14.

1 serving: 287 Calories; 13.8 g Total Fat; 1730 mg Sodium; 23 g Protein; 17 g Carbohydrate; trace Dietary Fiber

Pictured on page 53.

Tuna Biscuit Rolls

Tuna in a rolled up biscuit! Yummm.

Chopped onion	1/3 cup	75 mL
Diced red pepper	1/3 cup	75 mL
Hard margarine (or butter)	1 tbsp.	15 mL
Can of condensed Cheddar cheese soup	10 oz.	284 mL
Cans of chunk light tuna	2	2
(6 oz., 170 g, each), drained and broken up		
All-purpose flour	1 1/4 cups	300 mL
Whole wheat flour	1 cup	250 mL
Baking powder	4 tsp.	20 mL
Salt	1 tsp.	5 mL
Cooking oil	1/3 cup	75 mL
Milk	1 cup	250 mL
Milk	1/3 cup	75 mL

Sauté onion and red pepper in margarine in frying pan until softened. Remove from heat.

Stir in 1/2 of soup. Stir in tuna. Set aside.

Combine both flours, baking powder and salt in medium bowl. Add cooking oil. Mix until crumbly. Stir in first amount of milk until moistened. Turn out onto lightly floured surface. Knead 8 to 10 times. Roll out to 9 x 12 inch (22 x 30 cm) rectangle. Spread with tuna mixture. Roll up, jelly roll-style, from narrow end. Pinch seam closed. Cut into 6 slices. Carefully place in greased 9 x 13 inch (22 x 33 cm) pan. Bake, uncovered, in 400°F (205°C) oven for about 25 minutes until browned.

Combine remaining 1/2 of soup and second amount of milk in small saucepan. Stir to heat through. Pour over rolls. Makes 6 rolls.

1 roll: 442 Calories; 20.4 g Total Fat; 1021 mg Sodium; 20 g Protein; 46 g Carbohydrate; 4 g Dietary Fiber

(continued on next page)

HAM BISCUIT ROLLS: Omit tuna. Add 2 cans of flakes of ham
(6 1/2 oz., 184 g, each).

HAM AND MUSHROOM BISCUIT ROLLS: Omit tuna and Cheddar cheese
soup. Add 1 1/3 cups (325 mL) diced ham, 1 cup (250 mL) grated
Cheddar cheese and can of condensed cream of mushroom or celery soup
(10 oz., 284 mL).

Ham 'N' Pineapple

Ham meatballs in a pineapple sauce. Serve over rice.

Lean ground pork	1 lb.	454 g
Cooked ham, ground in food processor	1 lb.	454 g
Large eggs, fork-beaten	2	2
Milk	3/4 cup	175 mL
Whole wheat bread slices, made into crumbs	4	4
PINEAPPLE SAUCE		
Cans of pineapple tidbits, with juice (14 oz., 398 mL, each)	2	2
Cornstarch	2 tbsp.	30 mL
Brown sugar, packed	1 cup	250 mL
White vinegar	1/3 cup	75 mL
Ground ginger	2 tsp.	10 mL

Combine ground pork, ham, eggs, milk and bread crumbs in large bowl.
Shape into 1 1/2 inch (3.8 cm) balls. Place on greased large baking sheet.
Bake in 375°F (190°C) for 20 minutes until firm and browned. Remove to
paper towel to drain. Put into 3 quart (3 L) casserole. Makes about
60 meatballs.

Pineapple Sauce: Bring all 5 ingredients to a boil in small saucepan. Makes
2 1/2 cups (625 mL) sauce. Pour over meatballs. Cover. Bake in 350°F
(175°C) oven for 30 minutes. Serves 8.

*1 serving: 406 Calories; 11 g Total Fat; 879 mg Sodium; 21 g Protein; 57 g Carbohydrate;
2 g Dietary Fiber*

Linguine With Saucy Ham And Peas

Ham, peas, pasta—all three are agreeable to most children.
Use whole milk for a more creamy texture.

SAUCE		
Milk	1 1/2 cups	375 mL
All-purpose flour	3 tbsp.	50 mL
Salt	1/4 tsp.	1 mL
Garlic powder	1/8 tsp.	0.5 mL
Onion powder	1/8 tsp.	0.5 mL
Diced cooked ham	1 cup	250 mL
Frozen peas	1 cup	250 mL
Sour cream	1/3 cup	75 mL
Linguine pasta	8 oz.	225 g
Boiling water	12 cups	3 L
Salt	1 tbsp.	15 mL

Freshly grated Parmesan cheese (optional)

Sauce: Gradually whisk milk into flour in medium saucepan until smooth. Stir in salt, garlic powder and onion powder. Heat on medium, stirring occasionally, until boiling and thickened.

Stir in ham and peas. Bring to a boil. Stir in sour cream. Keep warm until serving. Makes 3 cups (750 mL) sauce.

Cook pasta in boiling water and salt in large uncovered pot or Dutch oven for 11 to 13 minutes until tender but firm. Drain. Transfer to large bowl. Toss with sauce.

Sprinkle with Parmesan cheese. Serves 4.

1 serving: 400 Calories; 8.9 g Total Fat; 767 mg Sodium; 20 g Protein; 59 g Carbohydrate; 3 g Dietary Fiber

Pictured on page 54.

Only Chicken Soup

It's not a lie—everything but the chicken is blended smooth!

Chopped onion	1 cup	250 mL
Chopped celery	1 cup	250 mL
Garlic clove, minced	1	1
Cooking oil	1 tbsp.	15 mL
Water	6 cups	1.5 L
Chopped carrot (about 2 medium)	1 cup	250 mL
Medium potatoes, peeled and cut into 8 chunks	2	2
Peeled diced zucchini	1 1/2 cups	375 mL
Boneless, skinless chicken breast halves (about 2)	8 oz.	225 g
Chicken bouillon powder	3 tbsp.	50 mL
Parsley flakes	2 tsp.	10 mL
Bay leaf	1	1
Alphabet pasta, uncooked (optional)	1/2 cup	125 mL

Sauté onion, celery and garlic in cooking oil in large uncovered pot or Dutch oven until onion is soft and clear.

Stir in remaining 9 ingredients. Cover. Simmer for 1 hour. Remove chicken to cutting board. Remove and discard bay leaf. Purée soup, in 2 batches, in blender or with hand blender until smooth. Return to pot. Cut chicken into bite-sized pieces. Return to soup. Makes 10 2/3 cups (2.7 L).

1 cup (250 mL): 75 Calories; 2.1 g Total Fat; 579 mg Sodium; 6 g Protein; 8 g Carbohydrate; 1 g Dietary Fiber

 Food that has freezer burn on it can still be eaten after removing any dried areas.

Alphabet Soup

Kids love to see what they can spell on their spoons!

Finely chopped onion	1/4 cup	60 mL
Diced celery	1/2 cup	125 mL
Margarine (or butter)	2 tsp.	10 mL
Cans of condensed chicken broth (10 oz., 284 mL, each)	2	2
Water	4 cups	1 L
Vegetable cocktail juice (such as V8)	2 cups	500 mL
Diced potato (about 1 small)	1 cup	250 mL
Frozen mixed vegetables	1 1/2 cups	375 mL
Bay leaf	1	1
Parsley flakes	1/2 tsp.	2 mL
Dried thyme leaves	1/4 tsp.	1 mL
Alphabet pasta, uncooked	2/3 cup	150 mL
Diced cooked chicken (or turkey), see Tip, page 65	1 cup	250 mL

Sauté onion and celery in margarine in large saucepan until onion is soft and clear.

Stir in next 8 ingredients. Bring to a boil.

Stir in pasta and chicken. Simmer, partially covered, for about 20 minutes until potato and pasta are tender. Remove and discard bay leaf. Makes 10 cups (2.5 L).

1 cup (250 mL): 128 Calories; 2.2 g Total Fat; 601 mg Sodium; 10 g Protein; 17 g Carbohydrate; 2 g Dietary Fiber

Pictured on page 35 and back cover.

Mom's Creamed Tomato Soup

Warms the body and the soul.

Chopped onion	1/2 cup	125 mL
Chopped celery	1/2 cup	125 mL
Margarine (or butter)	1 tbsp.	15 mL
Water	1 cup	250 mL
Cans of stewed tomatoes, with juice (14 oz., 398 mL, each)	2	2
Chicken (or vegetable) bouillon powder	1 tbsp.	15 mL
Granulated sugar	1/2 tsp.	2 mL
Pepper	1/8 tsp.	0.5 mL
Homogenized milk	1 cup	250 mL
All-purpose flour	2 tbsp.	30 mL

Cheddar cheese fish crackers (optional)

Sauté onion and celery in margarine in medium saucepan for about 4 minutes until onion is soft and clear.

Add water, tomatoes, bouillon powder, sugar and pepper. Bring to a boil. Reduce heat. Simmer, partially covered, for 30 minutes. Purée in blender or with hand blender until smooth. Return to saucepan.

Gradually whisk milk into flour in small bowl until smooth. Add to tomato mixture. Heat and stir on medium until boiling and slightly thickened. Ladle into individual soup bowls.

Top with crackers. Makes 5 cups (1.25 L).

1 cup (250 mL): 125 Calories; 4.7 g Total Fat; 891 mg Sodium; 4 g Protein; 19 g Carbohydrate; 2 g Dietary Fiber

 If a recipe calls for 1 cup (250 mL) cooked chicken and you don't have any, boil half a boneless, skinless chicken breast in small saucepan with 1 cup (250 mL) water for 15 minutes until no pink remains in chicken.

Cheesy Popcorn Soup

A cheesy soup, full of blended vegetables and topped with popcorn.
The nutritiousness is well disguised!

Chopped onion	1/3 cup	75 mL
Chopped celery (about 1 large rib)	1/2 cup	125 mL
Margarine (or butter)	2 tsp.	10 mL
Water	5 cups	1.25 L
Grated carrot (about 2 small)	1/2 cup	125 mL
Grated peeled zucchini (about 1 small)	1 cup	250 mL
Diced potato (about 1 small)	1 1/4 cups	300 mL
Diced seeded tomato (about 1 medium)	1 cup	250 mL
Bay leaf	1	1
Vegetable bouillon powder	2 tbsp.	30 mL
Dry mustard	1/2 tsp.	2 mL
Pepper	1/8 tsp.	0.5 mL
Light cream cheese, cut into 6 pieces	4 oz.	125 g
Grated light sharp Cheddar cheese	1/2 cup	125 mL
Popped popcorn (1 heaping tbsp., 15 mL, unpopped)	2 cups	500 mL

Sauté onion and celery in margarine in large saucepan for about 4 minutes until onion is soft and clear.

Add next 9 ingredients. Stir. Bring to a boil. Simmer, partially covered, for 15 minutes until vegetables are very soft. Remove and discard bay leaf.

Stir in both cheeses. Heat and stir on low until cream cheese is melted. Remove from heat. Purée, in 2 batches, in blender until smooth.

Return to saucepan. Heat on low. Do not boil. Ladle into individual soup bowls. Top with popcorn. Makes 8 cups (2 L).

1 cup (250 mL): 114 Calories; 5.7 g Total Fat; 667 mg Sodium; 5 g Protein; 11 g Carbohydrate; 2 g Dietary Fiber

Corn Chowder

Perfect warmer-upper on a cold winter day.

Finely chopped onion	1/2 cup	125 mL
Finely chopped celery	1/2 cup	125 mL
Margarine (or butter)	1 tbsp.	15 mL
Grated carrot (about 2 small)	1/2 cup	125 mL
Water	1 1/2 cups	375 mL
Chicken (or vegetable) bouillon powder	1 tsp.	5 mL
Parsley flakes	1 tsp.	5 mL
Pepper	1/4 tsp.	1 mL
Cans of cream-style corn (14 oz., 398 mL, each)	2	2
Milk	1 cup	250 mL

Sauté onion and celery in margarine in large saucepan until onion is soft and clear.

Stir in carrot, water, bouillon powder, parsley and pepper. Cover. Simmer for about 25 minutes until vegetables are soft and water is almost absorbed.

Stir in corn and milk. Bring to a boil. Makes 5 cups (1.25 L).

1 cup (250 mL): 182 Calories; 3.8 g Total Fat; 690 mg Sodium; 5 g Protein; 37 g Carbohydrate; 3 g Dietary Fiber

Variation: Add 1 cup (250 mL) chopped ham when adding corn and milk.

Paré Pointer

Why have history classes? We should let bygones be bygones.

Picnic Salad

This layered salad should be made the day before to allow the flavors to blend.

Iceberg lettuce (about 1 small), broken up	8 cups	2 L
Very thinly sliced red onion (about 1 small)	1/2 cup	125 mL
Can of sliced water chestnuts, well drained	8 oz.	227 mL
Red pepper (about 1 small), seeded and slivered into 2 inch (5 cm) pieces	1 cup	250 mL
Thinly sliced celery	1 cup	250 mL
Carrot (about 1 medium), pared into ribbons	1 cup	250 mL
Hard-boiled eggs, cooled, peeled and sliced	4 - 5	4 - 5
Frozen baby peas, thawed and drained	1 1/2 cups	375 mL
Light mayonnaise (not salad dressing)	2 cups	500 mL
Garlic and herb no-salt seasoning (such as Mrs. Dash)	1 1/2 tsp.	7 mL
Granulated sugar	1 tsp.	5 mL
Parsley flakes	1 tsp.	5 mL
Grated light sharp Cheddar cheese	2 cups	500 mL
Bacon slices, cooked crisp and crumbled	6	6
Small roma (plum) tomatoes, sliced	3	3

Layer first 8 ingredients, in order given, in 4 quart (4 L) clear bowl or 9 x 13 inch (22 x 33 cm) glass pan.

Combine mayonnaise, seasoning, sugar and parsley in small bowl. Spoon onto pea layer. Spread evenly up to edges of bowl to seal surface. Do not mix.

(continued on next page)

Soups & Salads

Sprinkle with cheese and bacon. Cover with plastic wrap. Chill for 8 to 24 hours.

To serve, arrange tomato slices on surface. Serves 10 to 12.

1 serving: 322 Calories; 21.8 g Total Fat; 670 mg Sodium; 12 g Protein; 19 g Carbohydrate; 3 g Dietary Fiber

Pictured on page 36.

Variation: Divide dressing in half. Spread 1/2 of dressing on red pepper layer and remaining 1/2 on top.

Dilled Carrots And Beans

This is great warm or cold.

Baby carrots	2 cups	500 mL
Water	1 cup	250 mL
Granulated sugar	1 tsp.	5 mL
Dill seed	1/2 tsp.	2 mL
Salt	1/2 tsp.	2 mL
Fresh whole green beans (see Note)	2 cups	500 mL
Non-fat Italian dressing	1/2 cup	125 mL
Dill weed	1/4 tsp.	1 mL

Combine carrots, water, sugar, dill seed and salt in medium saucepan. Bring to a boil. Reduce heat. Cover. Simmer for 5 minutes.

Add beans. Simmer for 5 minutes. Drain.

Add Italian dressing and dill weed. Toss to coat. Makes 4 cups (1 L).

1/2 cup (125 mL): 40 Calories; 0.2 g Total Fat; 284 mg Sodium; 1 g Protein; 9 g Carbohydrate; 2 g Dietary Fiber

Pictured on page 53.

Note: Omit fresh carrots and beans. Simmer same amount of frozen carrots and beans for 4 to 5 minutes. Drain. Add dressing and dill weed. Toss to coat.

Fruit Salad Dressing

The flavors of fresh fruit come alive with this tangy dressing.
Drizzle over fruit salad or serve in a small dish for dipping.

Plain yogurt	1 cup	250 mL
Liquid honey	3 tbsp.	50 mL

Combine both ingredients in small bowl. Makes about 1 cup (250 mL).

2 tbsp. (30 mL): 38 Calories; 0.4 g Total Fat; 20 mg Sodium; 1 g Protein; 8 g Carbohydrate; trace Dietary Fiber

Variation: Try adding 1 of the following: 1/2 tsp. (2 mL) cinnamon, 1 tsp. (5 mL) grated lemon peel, or 1 tbsp. (15 mL) instant chocolate drink mix.

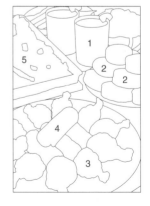

Teen Party

1. Orange Frost, page 148
2. Frozen Sandwiches, page 81
3. Drumsticks, page 28
4. Sausage Treats, page 104
5. Taco Cheese Fries, page 111

Props Courtesy Of: Le Gnome

Carrot And Raisin Salad

*If raisins are already soft, skip the plumping method and
combine carrot, raisins and salad dressing.*

Raisins	1/4 cup	60 mL
Water	1/3 cup	75 mL
Granulated sugar	1/2 tsp.	2 mL
Salt, sprinkle		
Lemon juice	1/2 tsp.	2 mL
Grated carrot	1 3/4 cups	425 mL
Light salad dressing	2 1/2 tbsp.	37 mL

Place raisins, water, sugar, salt and lemon juice in small saucepan. Simmer
for 5 minutes. Remove from heat. Let stand for about 15 minutes until
raisins are plump. Drain.

Combine carrot and salad dressing in small bowl. Stir in raisin mixture.
Makes 2 cups (500 mL).

*1/2 cup (125 mL): 79 Calories; 2.6 g Total Fat; 92 mg Sodium; 1 g Protein; 14 g Carbohydrate;
2 g Dietary Fiber*

Team Night
1. Candied Twists, page 136
2. Stacked Chili Wedges, page 44
3. Chocolate Fudge, page 131
4. Baked Salsa Cheese Dip, page 129

Props Courtesy Of: Stokes
                      Wal-Mart Canada Inc.

Chewy Wheat And Fruit Salad

Can be served the next day, but it will thicken. Thin with cereal cream until desired consistency is reached.

Can of pineapple tidbits, with juice	14 oz.	398 mL
Wheat	2/3 cup	150 mL
Water		
Salt	1/2 tsp.	2 mL
Lemon-flavored gelatin (jelly powder)	1 tbsp.	15 mL
Envelope of dessert topping (not prepared)	1	1
Cold water	1/4 cup	60 mL
Red seedless grapes, halved	1/2 cup	125 mL
Diced bananas	1/2 cup	125 mL
Fresh strawberries, sliced	1/2 cup	125 mL
Salt, sprinkle		
Small cantaloupes	2	2

Drain pineapple, reserving juice. Set pineapple aside. Chill juice.

Measure wheat into small saucepan. Add enough water to cover by 2 inches (5 cm). Add salt. Bring to a boil. Cover. Boil slowly for about 80 minutes until tender. Drain. Cool.

Measure 1/4 cup (60 mL) reserved pineapple juice into small saucepan. Bring to a boil. Stir in gelatin until dissolved. Cool until room temperature and partially thickened.

Empty dessert topping into medium bowl. Add 1/4 cup (60 mL) pineapple juice and cold water. Discard any remaining juice. Beat on high until soft peaks form. Still beating, add gelatin mixture. Beat until stiff.

Fold in pineapple, wheat mixture, grapes, bananas, strawberries and salt. Chill.

(continued on next page)

Cut cantaloupe in half crosswise. Scoop out seeds and discard. Cut rings 3/4 inch (2 cm) wide. Remove skin. Place ring on plate. Scoop salad into center of ring. Makes 4 cups (1 L).

3/4 cup (175 mL): 270 Calories; 4.4 g Total Fat; 37 mg Sodium; 5 g Protein; 58 g Carbohydrate; 6 g Dietary Fiber

Pictured on front cover.

Tomato Broccoli Casserole

A great way to disguise broccoli.

Frozen (or fresh) chopped broccoli	2 1/4 lbs.	1 kg
Water	2 cups	500 mL
Salt	1 tsp.	5 mL
Large eggs, fork-beaten	2	2
Can of condensed cream of mushroom soup	10 oz.	284 mL
Grated Cheddar cheese	1/2 cup	125 mL
Dried whole oregano	1/4 tsp.	1 mL
Can of stewed tomatoes, with juice, broken up	14 oz.	398 mL
Grated Parmesan cheese	2 tbsp.	30 mL

Combine broccoli in water and salt in large saucepan. Cover. Cook for about 3 minutes until tender-crisp. Drain well. Turn into greased 2 quart (2 L) casserole.

Combine eggs, soup, cheese, oregano and tomatoes in medium bowl. Pour over broccoli. Stir gently.

Sprinkle with Parmesan cheese. Bake, uncovered, in 350°F (175°C) oven for 45 minutes until hot and bubbly. Serves 8.

1 serving: 141 Calories; 7.5 g Total Fat; 563 mg Sodium; 9 g Protein; 13 g Carbohydrate; 5 g Dietary Fiber

Cheesy Cauliflower

At Halloween serve as Cheesy Brain Chunks.

Water	4 cups	1 L
Large head of cauliflower, trimmed and cut into florets	2 lbs.	900 g
Can of condensed Cheddar cheese soup	10 oz.	284 mL
Salad dressing (or mayonnaise)	1/4 cup	60 mL
Prepared mustard	1/2 tsp.	2 mL
Margarine (or butter)	1 tbsp.	15 mL
Fine dry bread crumbs	1/4 cup	60 mL

Bring water to a boil in large saucepan. Add cauliflower. Cover. Simmer for about 5 minutes until tender-crisp. Drain well. Turn into greased 1 1/2 quart (1.5 L) casserole.

Pour soup into small bowl. Stir until smooth. Add salad dressing and mustard. Stir until combined. Spoon onto cauliflower.

Melt margarine in small saucepan. Stir in crumbs. Sprinkle over cauliflower. Bake, uncovered, in 350°F (175°C) oven for about 25 minutes. Serves 6.

1 serving: 165 Calories; 11.6 g Total Fat; 523 mg Sodium; 4 g Protein; 12 g Carbohydrate; 1 g Dietary Fiber

Broccoli Trees

You can usually get fussier children to eat their vegetables if they can pick them up in their fingers.

Broccoli florets with 2 inch (5 cm) stems	1 lb.	454 g
Water		
Grated Parmesan cheese	2 tsp.	10 mL
Italian-flavored no-salt seasoning (such as Mrs. Dash)	1 tsp.	5 mL

(continued on next page)

Peel any thick fibrous skin from broccoli stem. Cut "trees" by separating florets with knife and slicing down through stem. Place in steamer over simmering water. Cover. Steam for 8 to 10 minutes until stems are tender and broccoli is bright green. Drain.

Combine Parmesan cheese and seasoning in small dish. Sprinkle over broccoli. Serves 6.

1 serving: 32 Calories; 0.9 g Total Fat; 60 mg Sodium; 3 g Protein; 4 g Carbohydrate; 2 g Dietary Fiber

Surprise Carrots

Just tell them it's carrots and they'll never know the turnip is there.

Carrots, peeled and cut into 1 inch (2.5 cm) chunks (about 5 – 6 medium)	1 lb.	454 g
Yellow turnip, peeled and diced (about 1 small)	1 lb.	454 g
Water	2 cups	500 mL
Margarine (or butter)	2 tbsp.	30 mL
Salt	1/2 tsp.	2 mL
Pepper	1/8 tsp.	0.5 mL

Place carrot, turnip and water in large saucepan. Bring to a boil on medium. Cook for about 25 minutes until tender. Drain, reserving 1/3 cup (75 mL) liquid in saucepan.

Add margarine, salt and pepper to liquid. Mash very well with potato masher or process in food processor until smooth. Makes 4 cups (1 L).

1/2 cup (125 mL): 65 Calories; 3.1 g Total Fat; 231 mg Sodium; 1 g Protein; 9 g Carbohydrate; 2 g Dietary Fiber

Green Flower Potatoes

Great at supper and the leftovers warm up well for lunch the next day.

Unpeeled medium baking potatoes (about 2 lbs., 900 g)	4	4
Cooking oil	2 tsp.	10 mL
Broccoli	3/4 lb.	340 g
Water		
Margarine (or butter), melted	1 tbsp.	15 mL
Process cheese spread	1/4 cup	60 mL
Grated light sharp Cheddar cheese	3/4 cup	175 mL
Salt	1/2 tsp.	2 mL
Onion powder	1/8 tsp.	0.5 mL
Pepper, sprinkle		
Pimiento pieces (optional)	8	8

Poke each potato in top with fork once or twice. Coat hands with cooking oil. Rub over each potato. Bake directly on center rack in 425°F (220°C) oven for 45 minutes until soft when poked with tip of sharp knife. Remove from oven. Cool enough to handle. Cut in half lengthwise. Carefully scoop flesh into medium bowl, leaving about 1/8 inch (3 mm) remaining in shell. Mash potato until only very small pieces remain.

Cut florets from broccoli. Peel and dice stems. Place stems in bottom of steamer basket. Add florets. Cover. Steam over simmering water for about 7 to 8 minutes until bright green and tender. Immediately rinse under cold running water until no longer warm. Drain well. Remove florets to small bowl. Add stems to mashed potato.

Stir in margarine, cheese spread, cheese, salt, onion powder and pepper. Divide evenly among shells. Shape into mounds over top of shell. Arrange florets, stem side down, in stuffing to form circle of flowers.

Place pimiento pieces in center. Cover. Chill until ready to heat. Place in single layer in roaster. Cover. Bake in 350°F (175°C) oven for 35 minutes until heated through. Makes 8 stuffed potatoes.

1 stuffed potato: 171 Calories; 6.7 g Total Fat; 407 mg Sodium; 7 g Protein; 21 g Carbohydrate; 2 g Dietary fiber

Seasoned Potato Wedges

Most young people will eat these—especially
when served with ketchup, mayonnaise or sour cream.

Unpeeled medium baking potatoes (about 2 lbs., 900 g)	4	4
Cooking oil	2 tbsp.	30 mL
Seasoned salt	1 tsp.	5 mL
Chili powder	1 tsp.	5 mL
Parsley flakes	1 tsp.	5 mL
Garlic powder	1/4 tsp.	1 mL
Pepper	1/4 tsp.	1 mL

Cut each potato into 10 to 12 wedges. Place in large bowl. Drizzle with cooking oil. Toss until coated. Arrange on greased 11 x 17 inch (28 x 43 cm) baking sheet.

Combine remaining 5 ingredients in small cup. Sprinkle over potatoes. Stir to coat. Bake on bottom rack in 450°F (230°C) oven for about 30 minutes, turning at half-time, until inside is tender and outside is crisp and lightly browned. Makes about 48 wedges.

4 wedges: 37 Calories; 2.4 g Total Fat; 117 mg Sodium; 1 g Protein; 4 g Carbohydrate; trace Dietary Fiber

Pictured on page 144.

Paré Pointer

The heat rises in the stadium once all the fans are gone.

Crumbly Potatoes

Easy and yummy.

Unpeeled medium baking potatoes (about 2 lbs., 900 g)	4	4
Cooking oil	2 tbsp.	30 mL
Cheddar cheese-flavored crackers, crumbled	30	30
Parsley flakes	1 tsp.	5 mL
Dill weed	1/2 tsp.	2 mL
Seasoned salt	1/2 tsp.	2 mL
Pepper	1/4 tsp.	1 mL
Cayenne pepper	1/8 tsp.	0.5 mL

Cut each potato into 1/4 inch (6 mm) slices. Place in large bowl. Drizzle with cooking oil. Toss until coated.

Combine remaining 6 ingredients in resealable freezer bag. Add potato slices, a few at a time. Shake until coated. Repeat until all potato slices are coated. Place on 11 x 17 inch (28 x 43 cm) greased baking sheet. Bake on bottom rack in 450°F (230°C) oven for about 35 minutes, turning at half-time, until inside is tender and outside is crisp and lightly browned. Makes 56 slices.

4 slices: 62 Calories; 3.4 g Total Fat; 117 mg Sodium; 1 g Protein; 7 g Carbohydrate; trace Dietary Fiber

Pictured on page 89.

 When a recipe calls for crushed crackers, you can chop them in a blender or food processor in no time.

Frozen Sandwiches

Like ice cream sandwiches, but with a pudding-type filling.
A big hit at birthday parties.

Instant chocolate pudding powder, 4 serving size	1	1
Envelope of dessert topping (not prepared)	1	1
Ground cinnamon	1/4 tsp.	1 mL
Cold milk	1 1/2 cups	375 mL
Vanilla	1 tsp.	5 mL
Round chocolate wafers	44	44
Chocolate (or colored candy) sprinkles (optional)		

Place first 5 ingredients in medium bowl. Beat on low speed until combined. Beat on high speed for about 5 minutes until thick. Makes 3 cups (750 mL) filling.

Place 2 tbsp. (30 mL) filling on 1/2 of wafers. Top with second 1/2 of wafers. Place candy sprinkles on waxed paper. Roll edges of sandwiches in sprinkles. Place on baking sheet. Freeze for 3 hours. Wrap individually in plastic wrap. Makes 22 sandwiches.

1 sandwich: 89 Calories; 2.8 g Total Fat; 109 mg Sodium; 2 g Protein; 15 g Carbohydrate; trace Dietary Fiber

Pictured on page 71.

FROZEN GRAHAM SANDWICHES: Omit chocolate wafers. Use 32 graham crackers. Divide and spread 3 tbsp. (50 mL) filling among half of graham crackers. Top with second half of graham crackers. Coat with candy sprinkles. Freeze. Makes 16 sandwiches.

Cheesecake Bundt

A different way of serving cheesecake to a large group.
Drizzle with either Strawberry Glaze, below, or Cranberry Glaze, page 83.

Hard margarine (or butter)	1/4 cup	60 mL
Liquid honey	2 tbsp.	30 mL
Graham cracker crumbs	1 1/2 cups	375 mL
Ground cinnamon	1/4 tsp.	1 mL
Ground nutmeg	1/4 tsp.	1 mL
Envelopes of unflavored gelatin (1/4 oz., 7 g, each)	3	3
Freshly squeezed lemon juice	1/3 cup	75 mL
Can of sweetened condensed milk	11 oz.	300 mL
Milk	1 cup	250 mL
Egg yolks (large), fork-beaten	3	3
Salt	1/2 tsp.	2 mL
Light cream cheese, softened and cut into 8 pieces	8 oz.	250 g
Grated lemon peel	2 tsp.	10 mL
Vanilla	1 tsp.	5 mL
Dry curd cottage cheese	3 cups	750 mL
Egg whites (large)	3	3
Granulated sugar	1/3 cup	75 mL
Whipping cream	1 1/2 cups	375 mL
STRAWBERRY GLAZE		
Container of frozen strawberries in syrup	15 oz.	425 g
Water, with syrup to equal	1 cup	250 mL
Cornstarch	4 tsp.	20 mL

(continued on next page)

Melt margarine and honey in small saucepan. Stir in graham crumbs, cinnamon and nutmeg. Reserve 1/3 cup (75 mL). Firmly press remaining into bottom and part way up sides of lightly greased 12 cup (2.7 L) bundt pan. Bake in 350°F (175°C) oven for 5 minutes until set. Cool.

Sprinkle gelatin over lemon juice in large saucepan. Let stand for 5 minutes. Heat on medium until gelatin is dissolved.

Stir in both milks, egg yolks and salt. Heat and stir on medium until thickened.

Whisk in cream cheese, lemon peel and vanilla until cheese is melted. Remove from heat.

Process cottage cheese in food processor or put through food mill until curds are very fine. Stir into milk mixture. Cool in refrigerator, stirring several times, until starting to thicken.

Beat egg whites in medium bowl until soft peaks form. Slowly beat in sugar until stiff and glossy.

Beat whipping cream in separate medium bowl until stiff peaks form. Transfer cottage cheese mixture to large bowl. Fold in egg whites, alternating with whipped cream. Pour into bundt pan. Smooth top. Sprinkle with reserved crumbs. Chill for several hours or overnight. To remove from pan, invert onto serving plate. Hold hot wet cloth over top and sides, reheating cloth several times, until cheesecake releases onto plate.

Strawberry Glaze: Strain juice from strawberries into 1 cup (250 mL) measure. Add water to equal 1 cup (250 mL). Reserve strawberries. Pour juice into small saucepan. Stir in cornstarch. Heat and stir on medium until boiling and thickened. Let cool slightly before stirring in reserved strawberries. Chill. Pour over cheesecake. Serves 12.

1 serving: 510 Calories; 23.6 g Total Fat; 553 mg Sodium; 17 g Protein; 60 g Carbohydrate; 1 g Dietary Fiber

Pictured on front cover.

CRANBERRY GLAZE: Combine 3 tbsp. (50 mL) granulated sugar and 1 tbsp. (15 mL) cornstarch in small saucepan. Stir in 1/4 cup (60 mL) water, 14 oz. (398 mL) can of whole cranberry sauce and 1/2 tsp. (2 mL) grated lemon peel. Heat and stir on medium until boiling and thickened. Chill. Pour over cheesecake. Serves 12.

Ice Cream Sundae Cake

Three kinds of ice cream and a fudgy cookie layer make this a decadent favorite.

CRUST

Package of cream-filled chocolate cookies	12 oz.	350 g
Hard margarine (or butter), melted	3 tbsp.	50 mL
Vanilla ice cream	2 cups	500 mL

FUDGE SAUCE

Hard margarine (or butter)	1/4 cup	60 mL
Granulated sugar	3/4 cup	175 mL
Cocoa	1/2 cup	125 mL
Whipping cream	1/2 cup	125 mL
Vanilla	1 tsp.	5 mL
Bananas, sliced lengthwise	3	3
Chocolate ice cream	2 cups	500 mL
Strawberry ice cream	2 cups	500 mL
Shaved chocolate curls, for garnish		
Whipping cream	1/2 cup	125 mL
Icing (confectioner's) sugar	2 tsp.	10 mL
Maraschino cherries, for garnish		

Crust: Process cookies in blender, in batches, until crushed. Reserve half.

Combine remaining half with margarine in small bowl. Line 10 inch (25 cm) springform pan with plastic wrap, letting some drape over sides of pan. Press crumb mixture into bottom of pan to make firm crust.

Stir vanilla ice cream in medium bowl until softened. Spread on crust evenly. Freeze until hard.

(continued on next page)

Desserts

Fudge Sauce: Melt margarine in medium saucepan. Stir in sugar and cocoa until combined. Add whipping cream. Heat and stir on medium until boiling. Remove from heat. Stir in vanilla. Cool to room temperature. Pour over vanilla ice cream layer.

Arrange banana on fudge sauce in single layer. Freeze for 1 hour until fudge sauce is firm.

Stir chocolate ice cream in medium bowl until softened. Spread evenly on banana layer. Sprinkle 1 cup (250 mL) of reserved cookies over ice cream. Pat down slightly. Freeze for 20 to 30 minutes.

Stir strawberry ice cream in medium bowl until softened. Spread evenly on cookie layer. Cover with plastic wrap. Freeze for about 3 hours until firm.

Invert, still covered, onto cutting board. Remove sides of pan. Remove plastic wrap from crust and sides. Invert serving plate over crust. Using plastic wrap underneath, and holding plate, turn cake over. Remove plastic wrap from top. Gently toss remaining cookie crumbs onto slightly melted sides and top. Sprinkle chocolate curls over surface. Beat whipping cream and icing sugar in small bowl. Pipe rosettes onto surface. Place 1 maraschino cherry in center of each rosette. Freeze, uncovered, until hard. Wrap in plastic wrap to store in freezer. Cuts into 16 wedges.

1 wedge: 374 Calories; 21.1 g Total Fat; 218 mg Sodium; 4 g Protein; 45 g Carbohydrate; 2 g Dietary Fiber

Pictured on page 54.

Variation: Omit bananas. Vary ice cream flavors as desired.

 To spread ice cream layer easily, spoon ice cream into pan. Cover with plastic wrap. Spread ice cream to edge with hands. Remove plastic wrap.

Chocolate Cookie Pretzels

Sweet instead of savory, but just as addicting.

Hard margarine (or butter), softened	1/2 cup	125 mL
Cream cheese, softened	8 oz.	250 g
Granulated sugar	1 1/4 cups	300 mL
Vanilla	1/2 tsp.	2 mL
Large egg	1	1
All-purpose flour	3 cups	750 mL
Cocoa	1/2 cup	125 mL
Baking powder	1/2 tsp.	2 mL
Salt	1/2 tsp.	2 mL
Semisweet chocolate baking squares (1 oz., 28 g, each)	1 - 2	1 - 2
White chocolate baking squares (1 oz., 28 g, each)	1 - 2	1 - 2

Beat margarine and cream cheese in large bowl until smooth. Beat in sugar and vanilla until combined. Beat in egg until light and fluffy.

Combine next 4 ingredients in medium bowl. Gradually beat into margarine mixture, kneading in last amount by hand until fairly stiff and no flour is visible. Shape into ball. Wrap in plastic wrap. Chill for 30 minutes until firm enough to handle. Roll about 2 tbsp. (30 mL) dough into pencil-thick ropes about 9 to 10 inches (22 × 25 cm) long. Form into pretzel shapes on large greased baking sheet about 2 inches (5 cm) apart. Bake on center rack in 350°F (175°C) oven for about 15 minutes until set. Remove to rack to cool.

Melt semisweet chocolate squares in small saucepan. Melt white chocolate squares in separate small saucepan. Drizzle separate chocolate colors onto warm cookies in a zigzag pattern in opposite directions. Makes 3 dozen pretzels.

1 pretzel: 134 Calories; 6.5 g Total Fat; 92 mg sodium; 2 g Protein; 18 g Carbohydrate; 1 g Dietary Fiber

Pictured on page 107.

Variation: Dip entire face of cookie in melted dark chocolate wafers. Sprinkle with white nuts, white chocolate or white candy.

All-Purpose Shortbread

This dough can be tinted, flavored and decorated, for any occasion, with candied fruit, chocolate chips, candy sprinkles or whatever happens to be in your cupboard.

Butter (not margarine), softened	1 1/2 cups	375 mL
Granulated sugar	1/2 cup	125 mL
Vanilla (or white vanilla)	1 tsp.	5 mL
All-purpose flour	3 cups	750 mL

Cream butter and sugar together until fluffy. Add vanilla. Mix. Gradually mix in flour until smooth. Chill for about 15 minutes until firm enough to handle. Roll 2 tbsp. (30 mL) dough into ropes. Shape into desired letters or numbers. Arrange on ungreased baking sheet. Bake in 325°F (160°C) oven for about 15 minutes until edges are just turning brown. Makes about 26 cookies.

1 cookie: 171 Calories; 11.4 g Total Fat; 115 mg Sodium; 2 g Protein; 16 g Carbohydrate; trace Dietary Fiber

CANDY CANES: Omit vanilla. Add peppermint flavoring. Tint half of dough with red food coloring. Twist 2 ropes together to form candy cane shape.

CUT-OUTS: Divide dough in half. Color 1/2 red. Color remaining 1/2 green. Roll out, 1 portion at a time, on lightly floured surface to 1/4 inch (6 mm) thick. Cut out with cookie cutter. Decorate with confetti cake decorations, balls, or sprinkles. Pictured on page 126.

VALENTINE HEARTS: Omit vanilla. Add cinnamon flavoring and red food coloring.

Note: To ensure a white cookie, use white vanilla.

Corn Flake Drop Cookies

Keep frozen dough on hand for a warm after-school snack.

Hard margarine (or butter), softened	1 1/2 cups	375 mL
Brown sugar, packed	1 2/3 cups	400 mL
Vanilla	2 tsp.	10 mL
Large eggs, fork-beaten	3	3
All-purpose flour	2 cups	500 mL
Whole wheat flour	1 cup	250 mL
Baking powder	2 tsp.	10 mL
Baking soda	1 tsp.	5 mL
Salt	1/2 tsp.	2 mL
Crushed corn flakes cereal	2 cups	500 mL

Cream margarine and sugar until fluffy. Stir in vanilla and eggs until mixed.

Combine both flours, baking powder, baking soda and salt in medium bowl. Gradually add to butter mixture, stirring after each addition, until well moistened.

Stir in cereal. Drop by mounded tablespoonfuls onto greased cookie sheet. Bake in 350°F (175°C) oven for about 11 minutes until light golden. Makes about 64 cookies.

1 cookie: 101 Calories; 4.9 g Total Fat; 132 mg Sodium; 1 g Protein; 13 g Carbohydrate; trace Dietary Fiber

Birthday

1. Fruit Mix Shake, page 145
2. Monster Snake Cake, page 96
3. No Beans! Chili, page 45
4. Crumbly Potatoes, page 80
5. Chip 'N' Chicken Strips, page 31

Coconut Macaroons

Soft and chewy with a golden crisp bottom.

White Angel Food cake mix	16 oz.	450 g
Large egg	1	1
Water	1/4 cup	60 mL
Hard margarine (or butter), melted	2 tbsp.	30 mL
Unsweetened medium coconut	2 cups	500 mL

Combine all 5 ingredients in large bowl until evenly moistened. Drop by level tablespoonfuls onto greased baking sheets 4 inches (10 cm) apart. Bake in 375°F (190°C) oven for 8 to 10 minutes until golden on bottom. Remove to rack to cool. Makes about 3 dozen cookies.

1 cookie: 86 Calories; 4 g Total Fat; 33 mg Sodium; 2 g Protein; 12 g Carbohydrate; trace Dietary Fiber

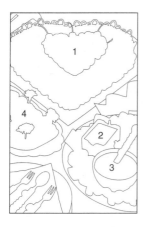

Sweet Sixteen

1. Cherry Heart Cake, page 98
2. Chocolate Dip, page 129
3. Honey Yogurt Dip, page 128
4. Saucy Meatballs, page 46

Props Courtesy Of: Call The Kettle Black

Paint-Box Cookies

Every cookie is different.

Hard margarine (or butter), softened	1 cup	250 mL
Granulated sugar	1 1/2 cups	375 mL
Liquid honey	1/4 cup	60 mL
Vanilla	2 tsp.	10 mL
Large eggs, fork-beaten	2	2
Baking soda	1 tbsp.	15 mL
Hot water	1 1/2 tbsp.	25 mL
All-purpose flour	4 1/2 cups	1.1 L
Liquid (or paste) food coloring (see Note)		

Cream margarine, sugar and honey together in large bowl. Stir in vanilla and eggs until well mixed.

Combine baking soda and water in small dish. Stir into margarine mixture.

Gradually add flour, mixing well after each addition, until dough is smooth. Divide into 4 or 5 portions. Add a few drops of food coloring to each portion, coloring each differently. Gently knead until coloring is evenly distributed. Divide each portion in half. Roll out each portion into ropes. Lay several ropes on top of each other. Twist gently into 1 rope. Roll out on lightly floured surface. Cut out with various cookie cutters (mix and match as desired). Place cookies on greased baking sheets, 1 inch (2.5 cm) apart. Bake in 350°F (175°C) oven for 8 to 10 minutes until cookies are set. Let cool before removing to rack. Makes about 6 dozen cookies.

1 cookie: 77 Calories; 2.9 g Total Fat; 83 mg Sodium; 1 g Protein; 12 g Carbohydrate; trace Dietary Fiber

Pictured on page 125.

Color suggestions: Easter – Pink, pale green, pale yellow, pale blue.

Halloween – Orange, black and plain.

Valentine – Red, pink and plain.

Christmas – Red, green and plain.

Note: Paste food coloring gives a wider variety of vivid colors. It can be purchased at craft or cake decorating stores.

Honey Cookies

Naturally delicious with roots in the Ukrainian culture.

Hard margarine (or butter), softened	1/4 cup	60 mL
Liquid honey	1/2 cup	125 mL
Large eggs	2	2
Light sour cream	1/2 cup	125 mL
Lemon flavoring	1/2 tsp.	2 mL
All-purpose flour	1 cup	250 mL
Whole wheat flour	1 cup	250 mL
Baking soda	1 tsp.	5 mL
Baking powder	1 tsp.	5 mL
Ground cinnamon	1/2 tsp.	2 mL
Salt	1/4 tsp.	1 mL
Roasted peanuts (or other nuts), optional		

Cream margarine and honey together. Add eggs, 1 at a time, beating well after each addition. Beat in sour cream and lemon flavoring.

Stir in both flours, baking soda, baking powder, cinnamon and salt. Mix well. Drop by tablespoonfuls onto greased baking sheet.

Press 1 or 2 peanuts into top of cookie. Bake in 350°F (175°C) oven for 10 minutes. Makes about 3 dozen cookies.

1 cookie: 54 Calories; 1.8 g Total Fat; 71 mg Sodium; 1 g Protein; 9 g Carbohydrate; 1 g Dietary Fiber

 Drop cookies require cool cookie sheets if you don't want them to spread.

Raisin Sandwich Cookies

An old-fashioned filled cookie that makes a nutritious and filling snack.
Note suggestion below for happy Jack-O-Lantern Cookies!

FILLING

Chopped dark raisins	1 1/2 cups	375 mL
Boiling water	1/2 cup	125 mL
Granulated sugar	1/4 cup	60 mL
Hard margarine (or butter)	2 tsp.	10 mL
Lemon juice	2 tsp.	10 mL
Salt	1/16 tsp.	0.5 mL
Margarine (or butter)	1 cup	250 mL
Granulated sugar	1 1/4 cups	300 mL
Milk	1 tbsp.	15 mL
Vanilla	1 tsp.	5 mL
Large eggs	2	2
All-purpose flour	2 cups	500 mL
Whole wheat flour	2/3 cup	150 mL
Baking powder	2 tsp.	10 mL
Salt	1/2 tsp.	2 mL
Ground cardamom	1/4 tsp.	1 mL

Filling: Combine all 6 ingredients in medium saucepan. Bring to a simmer on medium, stirring occasionally. Reduce heat to low. Cook for 10 to 12 minutes until thickened. Cool. Makes 1 cup (250 mL).

Cream margarine and sugar together in large bowl. Beat in milk, vanilla and eggs.

Stir in remaining 5 ingredients until well combined. Divide in half. Wrap each in plastic wrap. Chill for at least 2 hours. Turn out 1 portion onto lightly floured surface. Roll out to 1/8 inch (3 mm) thickness. Cut out 2 1/2 inch (6.4 cm) circles with round cutter. Place about 1 1/2 tsp. (7 mL) filling on 1/2 of circles, keeping 1/4 inch (6 mm) from edge. With remaining circles, make cut-outs, poke holes with fork or straw, or cut slits. Place on raisin filling. Seal edges with fork. Repeat with remaining dough. Bake on ungreased baking sheet in 375°F (190°C) oven for 10 to 12 minutes until golden. Remove to rack to cool. Makes about 3 dozen cookies.

(continued on next page)

Desserts

JACK-O-LANTERN COOKIES: Add a few drops of orange food coloring to milk mixture before adding dry ingredients. Prepare cookies as above, making cut out faces.

Pictured on page 143.

Mud Pie Sandwich

This is an easy dessert to make using ice cream sandwiches.
Stores in freezer for up to two months!

Ice cream sandwiches	24	24
(2 x 6 inch, 5 x 15 cm, each)		
Jar of fudge ice cream topping	1 cup	250 mL
Envelope of dessert topping	1	1
(not prepared)		
Chocolate instant pudding powder	4 oz.	113 g
(4 serving size)		
Cold milk	1 1/2 cups	375 mL
Chunky peanut butter	1/2 cup	125 mL
Semisweet chocolate chips, melted	1/3 cup	75 mL
Chopped peanuts	1/3 cup	75 mL

Line 9 x 13 inch (22 x 33 cm) pan with foil. Arrange 12 ice cream sandwiches in single layer in bottom of pan. Cover with 1/2 of fudge topping. Place in freezer.

Beat dessert topping, pudding and milk in medium bowl on high speed for about 5 minutes until thick and creamy. Beat in peanut butter. Spread 1/2 of peanut butter mixture on fudge topping layer. Arrange remaining 12 ice cream sandwiches in single layer. Cover with remaining fudge topping and chocolate filling.

Melt chocolate chips in small saucepan on low. Drizzle onto chocolate filling layer. Sprinkle with peanuts. Freeze for several hours. To store in freezer, remove from pan in foil liner. Wrap well in plastic wrap. Cuts into 15 pieces.

Monster Snake Cake

Root beer flavored cake in the shape of a snake.

White cake mix (2 layer size)	1	1
Flat root beer (see Note)	1 1/4 cups	300 mL
Large eggs	2	2
Cooking oil	1/4 cup	60 mL
FROSTING		
Envelopes of dessert topping (not prepared)	2	2
Package of vanilla instant pudding powder (4 serving size)	1	1
Milk	1 1/2 cups	375 mL
Yellow liquid food coloring		
DECORATION		
Thin red licorice strip (2 inches, 5 cm, long)	1	1
Candy corn	4	4
Gumdrop candy (various colors)	90	90
Black jelly bean candies	16	16
Doughnut-shaped hard candies (such as Lifesavers), same amount as birthday candles		

Spray bottoms of 2 round 8 inch (20 cm) cake pans with no-stick cooking spray. Line with waxed paper. Spray pan and paper with no-stick cooking spray. Beat cake mix, root beer, eggs and cooking oil in large bowl for 2 to 3 minutes until smooth. Divide between pans. Bake in 350°F (175°C) oven for about 30 minutes until wooden pick inserted in center comes out clean. Cool. Turn out onto flat surface. Remove waxed paper. Cut 3 1/4 inch (8 cm) circle in center of each cake. Leave in place. Cut both cakes in half, making a total of 4 C-shaped pieces (see Diagram 1) and 4 semi-circles (see Diagram 1). Cover cake board or heavy cardboard with foil. Arrange C-shaped pieces end to end, alternating directions to make curvy snake. Place 2 semi-circles, cut sides together, at one end of snake to make tail. Place remaining 2 semi-circles at other end of snake, slightly apart, to make open mouth(see Diagram 2).

(continued on next page)

Frosting: Beat dessert topping, pudding and milk in medium bowl until stiff peaks form. Beat in food coloring. Frost cut sides first with thin layer to seal in crumbs on cut edges. Frost where pieces are joined. Frost entire cake, making surface smooth and rounded.

Decoration: Split licorice strip halfway through for forked tongue. Place in mouth. Arrange candy corn in mouth for fangs. Arrange gumdrops and jelly beans on top and sides of cake for scales. Place birthday candles in center of doughnut-shaped candies on top of cake. Cuts into 16 pieces.

1 piece: 253 Calories; 10.4 g Total Fat; 167 mg Sodium; 3 g Protein; 37 g Carbohydrate; trace Dietary Fiber

Pictured on page 89.

Note: To make root beer flat, stir rapidly until bubbles no longer rise to the surface.

Variation: Omit vanilla instant pudding powder. Add same size pistachio pudding powder.

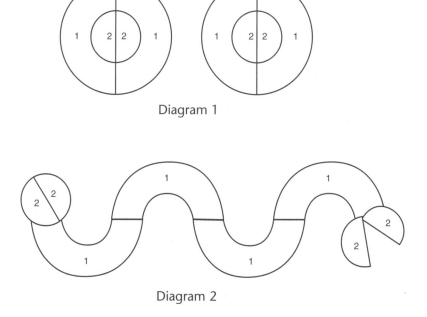

Diagram 1

Diagram 2

Cherry Heart Cake

Use this for a girl's Sweet Sixteen birthday or a special valentine.
Rich Cream Frosting, this page, is also good on Baby Butterfly Cakes, page 102.

White cake mix (2 layer size)	1	1
Maraschino cherry syrup	1/2 cup	125 mL
Milk	3/4 cup	175 mL
Cooking oil	1/3 cup	75 mL
Large eggs	3	3
Almond flavoring	1/2 tsp.	2 mL
RICH CREAM FROSTING		
Unflavored gelatin	1 tsp.	5 mL
Maraschino cherry syrup	2 tbsp.	30 mL
Whipping cream	2 cups	500 mL
Salt, just a pinch		
Icing (confectioner's) sugar (optional)	2 tbsp.	30 mL
Red liquid food coloring (optional)		

Maraschino cherries, well-drained (for garnish)
Chocolate filigrees, for garnish
Chocolate curls, for garnish

Line bottom of 9 x 9 inch (22 x 22 cm) square pan and 9 inch (22 cm) round pan with waxed paper. Spray with no-stick cooking spray. Slowly beat cake mix, syrup, milk, cooking oil, eggs and almond flavoring together until moistened. Beat for about 2 minutes until smooth. Divide between pans. Bake in 350°F (175°C) oven for 25 to 30 minutes until wooden pick inserted in center comes out clean. Cool on racks. Turn out. Peel off waxed paper. Cut round cake in half. Place square cake on foil-lined cake board or heavy cardboard to form, diamond shape. Place cut sides of round cake on adjacent sides of square cake to form heart shape (see Diagram, page 99). Trim top of cake to make flat.

Rich Cream Frosting: Stir gelatin into syrup in microwave-safe small bowl. Microwave on medium (50%) for 2 minutes until gelatin is dissolved. Let cool slightly.

(continued on next page)

Beat whipping cream in large bowl until soft peaks form. Add salt, icing sugar and food coloring. Slowly beat in gelatin mixture until stiff peaks form. Makes 4 cups (1 L) frosting.

Frost with thin layer of frosting to seal in crumbs on cut edge. Frost with thick layer. Garnish with cherries, chocolate filigrees and candy sprinkles. Serves 18.

1 serving: 304 Calories; 17.6 g Total Fat; 142 mg Sodium; 3 g Protein; 34 g Carbohydrate; trace Dietary Fiber

Pictured on page 90.

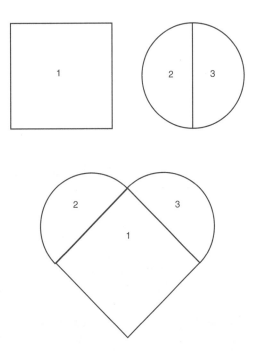

Banana Cake

Frost with Peanut Butter Frosting, page 101, for a classic combination — peanut butter and banana. Top with Spiderwebs, page 137, for a Halloween party.

Hard margarine (or butter), softened	3/4 cup	175 mL
Brown sugar, packed	1/2 cup	125 mL
Granulated sugar	1/2 cup	125 mL
Vanilla	2 tsp.	10 mL
Large eggs	2	2
All-purpose flour	2 cups	500 mL
Baking soda	1 tsp.	5 mL
Baking powder	1/2 tsp.	2 mL
Salt	1/2 tsp.	2 mL
1% buttermilk (see Tip, page 23)	3/4 cup	175 mL
Mashed ripe banana (about 2 medium)	1 cup	250 mL
Peanut Butter Frosting, page 101	3 1/2 cups	875 mL
Jelly bean candies	12 - 14	12 - 14

Beat margarine and both sugars in large bowl for about 2 minutes until light and fluffy. Beat in vanilla. Add eggs, 1 at a time, beating well after each addition.

Combine next 4 ingredients in small bowl.

Combine buttermilk and banana in separate small bowl. Add flour mixture to margarine mixture in 3 additions, alternating with banana mixture in 2 additions, beginning and ending with flour mixture. Pour into 2 greased 9 inch (22 cm) round pans or 9 x 13 inch (22 x 33 cm) pan. Bake in 350°F (175°C) oven for 30 minutes until wooden pick inserted in center comes out clean. Cool in pan for 10 minutes before turning out onto rack to cool completely.

Frost top and sides with frosting. Pipe frosting around edges. Place jelly bean candies randomly along edge and top. Serves 24.

1 serving: 150 Calories; 6.8 g Total Fat; 201 mg Sodium; 2 g Protein; 20 g Carbohydrate; 1 g Dietary Fiber

Pictured on page 143.

Peanut Butter Frosting

A creamy frosting that is very easy to prepare and holds well.
Subtle peanut flavor and not too sweet. Good on Banana Cake, page 100. Enough
to ice a 9 x 13 inch (22 x 33 cm) cake or a 2 layer 9 inch (22 cm) round cake.

Envelopes of dessert topping (not prepared)	2	2
Vanilla instant pudding powder (4 serving size)	4 oz.	102 g
Cold milk	1 1/2 cups	375 mL
Smooth peanut butter	1/3 cup	75 mL

Beat dessert topping, pudding and milk together in medium bowl for 3 to 4 minutes until almost thickened.

Beat in peanut butter until desired spreading consistency. Makes 3 1/2 cups (875 mL).

2 tbsp. (30 mL): 54 Calories; 2.8 g Total Fat; 35 mg Sodium; 1 g Protein; 6 g Carbohydrate; trace Dietary Fiber

Pictured on page 143.

VANILLA FROSTING: Omit peanut butter.

Paré Pointer
He never saw the Catskill Mountains but he saw cats kill mice.

Baby Butterfly Cupcakes

These look so pretty dusted with icing sugar and arranged on a platter.
Uses one half recipe of Rich Cream Frosting, page 98.

Hard margarine (or butter), softened	1/2 cup	125 mL
Granulated sugar	3/4 cup	175 mL
Vanilla (white is best)	1 tsp.	5 mL
Large eggs	2	2
All-purpose flour	1 3/4 cups	425 mL
Baking powder	1 1/2 tsp.	7 mL
Salt	1/8 tsp.	0.5 mL
Milk	3/4 cup	175 mL
Tiny colored seed candies	3 tbsp.	50 mL
Rich Cream Frosting, page 98 (1/2 recipe)		
Thin red licorice strips, for garnish	2 - 3	2 - 3
Icing (confectioner's) sugar, for garnish		

Beat margarine and sugar until light and fluffy. Beat in vanilla. Add eggs, 1 at a time, beating well after each addition.

Sift flour, baking powder and salt together in small bowl.

Add flour mixture to batter in 3 additions alternately with milk in 2 additions, beating on low until just mixed.

Fold in candies. Line muffin cups with medium-sized liners. Fill individual cups about 3/4 full. Bake on center rack in 400°F (205°C) oven for about 20 minutes until golden and wooden pick inserted in center comes out clean. Cool.

Cut a circle in top with pointed knife slightly angled to middle of cupcake, leaving 1/4 inch (6 mm) edge. Remove cone-shaped piece. Fill center with frosting. Cut cone tops in half. Arrange on frosting, rounded sides out, to form butterfly wings. Place 2 inch (5 cm) licorice strips in frosting to form antennae. Dust with icing sugar. Makes 12 cupcakes.

1 cupcake: 220 Calories; 9.4 g Total Fat; 147 mg Sodium; 4 g Protein; 30 g Carbohydrate; 1 g Dietary Fiber

Pictured on page 53.

Raspberry Cupcakes

A hint of chocolate with the raspberry flavor. Perfect!

White cake mix (2 layer size)	1	1
Cocoa	1/4 cup	60 mL
Large eggs	3	3
Cooking oil	1/3 cup	75 mL
Frozen concentrated raspberry juice	1/2 cup	125 mL
Water	7/8 cup	200 mL
BUTTER ICING		
Hard margarine (or butter), softened	1/3 cup	75 mL
Icing (confectioner's) sugar	2 cups	500 mL
Frozen concentrated raspberry juice	2 tbsp.	30 mL
Assorted candies, for garnish	20 - 22	20 - 22

Beat cake mix, cocoa, eggs, cooking oil, juice and water, for about 3 minutes, on medium until smooth. Line muffin cups with large-sized liners. Fill each cup 3/4 full. Bake in 350°F (175°C) oven for 15 to 17 minutes. Cool for 10 minutes in pan. Turn out onto racks to cool.

Butter Icing: Beat margarine until light and fluffy. Gradually add icing sugar, beating well after each addition. Add juice. Beat until smooth. Ice cupcakes. Top with candy. Makes about 20 cupcakes.

1 cupcake: 250 Calories; 10.8 g Total Fat; 142 mg Sodium; 2 g Protein; 38 g Carbohydrate; 1 g Dietary Fiber

Pictured on page 36.

Paré Pointer
It is rumored that basketball is played in Hawaii with hula hoops.

Sausage Treats

Serve these with salsa or mustard for dipping.

White (or whole wheat) bread slices, crusts removed	4	4
Margarine (or butter), melted	4 tsp.	20 mL
Process cheese spread	4 tsp.	20 mL
Frozen brown-and-serve sausages, thawed (or small sausages, cooked), see Note	4	4

Thinly roll out bread slices. Brush 1 side of each slice with 1 tsp. (5 mL) margarine. Spread other side of each slice with 1 tsp. (5 mL) cheese spread. Place sausage on cheese. Roll up bread, jelly roll-style. Place, seam side down, on ungreased baking sheet. Bake in 425°F (220°C) oven for 10 minutes until toasted. For one-bite size, cut each roll into 3 pieces. Makes 12 whole sausage treats, or 36 bite-size treats.

1 whole sausage treat: 57 Calories; 3.4 g Total Fat; 124 mg Sodium; 2 g Protein; 5 g Carbohydrate; trace Dietary Fiber

Pictured on page 71.

Note: For very young children, cut sausages in half lengthwise to avoid choking.

Sesame Snacks

This no-bake treat is just like those snacks you buy at the store.

Brown sugar, packed	1/2 cup	125 mL
Liquid honey	1/3 cup	75 mL
Toasted sesame seeds	2 cups	500 mL

(continued on next page)

Stir brown sugar and honey in medium saucepan on low until almost boiling and sugar is dissolved. Add sesame seeds. Stir until thick paste-like consistency. Turn out onto foil-lined 12 x 20 inch (30 x 50 cm) baking sheet. Cover with sheet of foil. Roll out to 1/4 inch (6 mm) thick. Peel back top layer of foil. Score 1 x 2 inch (2.5 x 5 cm) lines with wet sharp knife while still warm. Let stand, uncovered, for about 1 hour until cool and hardened. Break apart on score marks with knife. To make smaller pieces, break by hand. Makes about 37 sesame snacks.

1 sesame snack: 70 Calories; 4.1 g Total Fat; 4 mg Sodium; 1 g Protein; 8 g Carbohydrate; 1 g Dietary Fiber

Sombreros

These appetizers hold their shape well and have a mild Mexican flavor.

Light cream cheese, room temperature	8 oz.	250 g
Finely diced green pepper	1/4 cup	60 mL
Finely diced red pepper	1/3 cup	75 mL
Finely sliced green onion	1/4 cup	60 mL
Grated Monterey Jack with Jalapeño cheese	1 1/2 cups	375 mL
Finely diced cooked chicken (or turkey)	1 cup	250 mL
Favorite Salsa, page 130 (or commercial)	3 tbsp.	50 mL
Whole wheat (or sun-dried tomato) tortillas (10 inch, 25 cm, size)	5	5

Combine first 7 ingredients in small bowl. Makes 3 cups (750 mL) filling.

Divide and spread filling on tortillas. Roll up tightly, jelly roll-style. Wrap in plastic wrap. Chill for several hours or overnight. Remove plastic wrap. Place on greased baking sheet. Bake in 350°F (175°C) oven for 20 minutes until hot and cheese is starting to melt. Let sit for 5 minutes before cutting. Cut each roll into 5 pieces. Makes 25 appetizers.

1 appetizer: 88 Calories; 4.4 g Total Fat; 230 mg Sodium; 6 g Protein; 7 g Carbohydrate; 1 g Dietary Fiber

Mini Pups

*You'll have all the kids in the neighborhood
drooling at your door once they get a taste of these puppies!*

Hot dog buns	2	2
Process cheese slices	8	8
Wieners	2	2

Split each bun in half lengthwise. Cut each in half crosswise. Lay 1 slice of cheese loaf on each piece. Cut wiener in half crosswise. Cut in half lengthwise. Lay 1 piece on each cheese slice. Place on baking sheet or broiler pan. Broil about 5 inches (12.5 cm) from heat for 3 minutes until wiener is hot and cheese is melted. Makes 8 mini pups.

2 mini pups: 220 Calories; 13.7 g Total Fat; 775 mg Sodium; 10 g Protein; 14 g Carbohydrate; trace Dietary Fiber

Kindergarten

1. Traffic Lights, page 132
2. Butterscotch Puffed Wheat Squares, page 122
3. Chocolate Cookie Pretzels, page 86
4. Rainbow Ribbons, page 140

Props Courtesy Of: Wal-Mart Canada Inc.

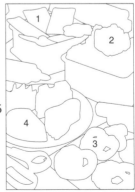

Taco Snack Mix

A spicy alternative to the usual Nuts 'N' Bolts.

Spoon-size shredded wheat cereal, unsweetened	3 cups	750 mL
Rice squares cereal (such as Crispix)	3 cups	750 mL
Corn chips	2 cups	500 mL
Stick pretzels, broken up	2 cups	500 mL
Unsalted peanuts	1 cup	250 mL
Hard margarine (or butter)	1/2 cup	125 mL
Envelope of salt-reduced taco seasoning mix	1 1/4 oz.	35 g

Combine first 5 ingredients in large roaster.

Melt margarine in small saucepan. Stir in seasoning mix. Drizzle over cereal mixture, tossing until coated. Bake in 350°F (175°C) oven for 30 minutes, stirring every 10 minutes, until toasted. Makes 11 cups (2.75 L).

1 cup (250 mL): 348 Calories; 20.1 g Total Fat; 685 mg Sodium; 7 g Protein; 37 g Carbohydrate; 4 g Dietary Fiber

Pictured on page 36.

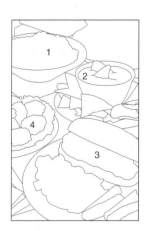

Video Night

1. Maple Nut Popcorn, page 112
2. Favorite Salsa, page 130
3. Meatball Heroes, page 26
4. Cheese Pinwheels, page 32

Props Courtesy Of: Wal-Mart Canada Inc.

Fried Cheese Balls

These are good warm or at room temperature.

Water	2 cups	500 mL
Uncooked brown rice	1 cup	250 mL
Seasoned salt	1 tsp.	5 mL
Onion powder	1/8 tsp.	0.5 mL
Garlic powder (optional)	1/8 tsp.	0.5 mL
Parsley flakes	1 tsp.	5 mL
Grated sharp Cheddar cheese	2 cups	500 mL
Large eggs, fork-beaten	2	2
Milk	1 tbsp.	15 mL
Finely crushed corn flakes cereal	1 1/2 cups	375 mL

Cooking oil, for deep frying

Bring water to a boil in medium saucepan. Add brown rice, seasoned salt, onion powder, garlic powder and parsley flakes. Reduce heat. Simmer for about 50 minutes until tender.

Stir in cheese until melted. Cool enough to handle.

Combine eggs and milk in small bowl.

Place cereal in separate small bowl.

Form cheese mixture into 1 1/4 inch (3 cm) balls. Drop into egg mixture to coat, then roll in cereal to coat. Fry in 375°F (190°C) cooking oil for 1 to 2 minutes until golden. Remove with slotted spoon to paper towel to drain. Makes 46 cheese balls.

1 cheese ball: 59 Calories; 2.8 g Total Fat; 97 mg Sodium; 2 g Protein; 6 g Carbohydrate; trace Dietary Fiber

Pictured on page 54.

Taco Cheese Fries

Great for sleepovers.

Frozen french fries	2 1/4 lbs.	1 kg
Taco seasoning mix (stirred before measuring)	1 tbsp.	15 mL
Chopped green onion	1/4 cup	60 mL
Seeded diced tomato	1/2 cup	125 mL
Diced red, green or yellow pepper	1/4 cup	60 mL
Can of condensed Cheddar cheese soup	10 oz.	284 mL
Milk	1/2 cup	125 mL
Cayenne pepper	1/8 tsp.	0.5 mL

Bake french fries on foil-lined 11 x 17 inch (28 x 43 cm) cookie sheet in 450°F (230°C) oven for 15 minutes.

Sprinkle with seasoning mix, onion, tomato and pepper. Mix.

Whisk soup, milk and cayenne pepper in 2 cup (500 mL) glass measure until smooth. Drizzle over fries evenly. Bake in 450°F (230°C) oven for about 10 minutes until bubbling around edges. Serves 6.

1 serving: *461 Calories; 19.4 g Total Fat; 1108 mg Sodium; 9 g Protein; 66 g Carbohydrate; 6 g Dietary Fiber*

Pictured on page 71.

 If you need to peel a tomato, make four shallow cuts just through the skin lengthwise from the stem. Put the tomato into boiling water for 30 seconds. Remove. Slip off the skin.

Maple Nut Popcorn

The taste of nuts and cranberries comes through.

Popcorn kernels	1/3 cup	75 mL
Pecans, broken and toasted	1 1/2 cups	375 mL
Dried cranberries	3/4 cup	175 mL
Hard margarine (or butter)	3/4 cup	175 mL
Maple-flavored pancake syrup	1 1/2 cups	375 mL
Golden corn syrup	2/3 cup	150 mL
Ground ginger	1/2 tsp.	2 mL
Ground cinnamon	1/2 tsp.	2 mL
Ground cloves	1/16 tsp.	0.5 mL
Maple flavoring	1 tsp.	5 mL

Pop kernels in hot air popper into very large bowl.

Add next 2 ingredients. Toss.

Melt margarine in large heavy saucepan. Stir in both syrups. Boil for about 20 minutes until soft-crack stage (separates into hard but pliable threads) or 275°F (140°C) on candy thermometer.

Add remaining 4 ingredients. Stir until well coated. Turn out onto 2 greased baking sheets. Spread into smaller clumps to cool. Makes 14 cups (3.5 L).

1/2 cup (125 mL): 177 Calories; 9.9 g Total Fat; 69 mg Sodium; 1 g Protein; 23 g Carbohydrate; 1 g Dietary Fiber

Pictured on page 108.

Variation: For a crispier snack, bake in 250°F (120°C) oven for 1 hour, stirring every 15 minutes.

Paré Pointer

A fourth grader wrote, "The only thing to do with a green alien is to wait until it ripens."

Colored Popcorn

The popcorn can be flavored and colored
any way you like for any kids' occasion.

Popcorn kernels	1/2 cup	125 mL
Granulated sugar	1 1/2 cups	375 mL
White corn syrup	1/3 cup	75 mL
Hard margarine (or butter)	1/2 cup	125 mL
Water	1/4 cup	60 mL
Package of flavored gelatin (jelly powder), any flavor	3 oz.	85 g

Pop kernels in hot air popper into very large bowl.

Combine next 4 ingredients in large saucepan. Bring to a slow boil. Boil for 3 1/2 minutes. Remove from heat.

Add flavored gelatin. Stir until sugar and gelatin are dissolved. Drizzle over popcorn, tossing until coated. Spread on lightly greased baking sheet. Bake in 250°F (120°C) oven for 40 minutes, stirring and breaking up clumps every 10 minutes. Makes 12 cups (3 L).

1 cup (250 mL): 261 Calories; 8.6 g Total Fat; 123 mg Sodium; 2 g Protein; 46 g Carbohydrate; 0 g Dietary Fiber

Pictured on page 125.

Paré Pointer

When a student misses the bus, he catches it when he gets home.

Cheese Popcorn

Two kinds of cheese make this popcorn extra delicious.

Popcorn kernels	1/2 cup	125 mL
Powdered Cheddar cheese product	2 tbsp.	30 mL
Grated Parmesan (or Romano) cheese	2 tbsp.	30 mL
Seasoned salt	1/2 tsp.	2 mL
Hard margarine (or butter), melted	1/4 cup	60 mL

Pop kernels in hot air popper into very large bowl.

Combine next 4 ingredients in small dish. Drizzle over popcorn, tossing until coated. Makes 14 cups (3.5 L).

1 cup (250 mL): 66 Calories; 4.1 g Total Fat; 120 mg Sodium; 2 g Protein; 6 g Carbohydrate; 0 g Dietary Fiber

Barbecued Popcorn

Great flavor and affordable enough to serve a large group of friends.

Popcorn kernels	1/2 cup	125 mL
Hard margarine (or butter), melted	1/4 cup	60 mL
Barbecue sauce	1 tbsp.	15 mL
Seasoned salt	1/2 tsp.	2 mL
Cayenne pepper (optional)	1/16 tsp.	0.5 mL

Pop kernels in hot air popper into very large bowl.

Combine next 4 ingredients. Drizzle over popcorn, tossing until coated. Makes 14 cups (3.5 L).

1 cup (250 mL): 58 Calories; 3.6 g Total Fat; 96 mg Sodium; 1 g Protein; 6 g Carbohydrate; trace Dietary Fiber

Snack Candy Mix

The more you eat the more you like it. Store in a sealed container.

Puffed rice cereal	2 cups	500 mL
Puffed wheat cereal	2 cups	500 mL
Rolled oats (not instant)	2 cups	500 mL
Sweetened flake coconut	1 cup	250 mL
Roasted shelled sunflower seeds	1/2 cup	125 mL
Cooking oil	1/2 cup	125 mL
Liquid honey	1/2 cup	125 mL
Skim milk powder	1/4 cup	60 mL
Cocoa	1/4 cup	60 mL
Ground cinnamon	1 tsp.	5 mL

Combine first 5 ingredients in very large bowl.

Heat and stir cooking oil and honey in small saucepan on medium until boiling. Remove from heat.

Process skim milk powder in blender until fine powder. Gradually stir into honey mixture with cocoa and cinnamon until thick and smooth. Drizzle, over cereal mixture, tossing until coated. Spread on 2 large baking sheets. Bake in 275°F (140°C) oven for about 30 minutes, stirring twice. Cool. Makes 9 2/3 cups (2.4 L).

1 cup (250 mL): 347 Calories; 19.4 g Total Fat; 41 mg Sodium; 7 g Protein; 41 g Carbohydrate; 4 g Dietary Fiber

 To get fewer unpopped kernels, store popcorn in the freezer until ready to use.

Applets

Looking for a candy-type gift?
This makes a great take-along when going to visit.

Cornstarch	2 tbsp.	30 mL
Granulated sugar	1/2 cup	125 mL
Water	1 - 2 tbsp.	15 - 30 mL
Envelopes unflavored gelatin	2	2
(1/4 oz., 7 g, each)		
Package of lemon-flavored gelatin	3 oz.	85 g
(jelly powder)		
Can of unsweetened applesauce	14 oz.	398 mL
Finely chopped walnuts	1/2 cup	125 mL

Icing (confectioner's) sugar, for coating

Stir cornstarch, sugar, water and both gelatins together well in medium saucepan. Add applesauce. Heat and stir until sugar and gelatin are dissolved.

Stir in walnuts. Pour into greased foil-lined 9 x 9 inch (22 x 22 cm) pan. Let stand overnight.

Place icing sugar in small bowl. Cut gelatin mixture into 9 squares. Roll individual square in icing sugar. Makes 48 squares.

1 square: 28 Calories; 0.9 g Total Fat; 6 mg Sodium; 1 g Protein; 5 g Carbohydrate; trace Dietary Fiber

PEACHLETS: Omit lemon-flavored gelatin (jelly powder), applesauce and walnuts. Purée two 14 oz. (398 mL) cans of sliced peaches, with juice, in blender. Pour into medium saucepan. Add cornstarch, sugar and water and 1 package (3 oz., 85 g) of peach-flavored gelatin (jelly powder). Heat and stir until sugar and gelatin are dissolved. Pour into greased foil-lined 8 x 8 inch (20 x 20 cm) pan. Proceed as above.

(continued on next page)

PEARLETS: Omit lemon-flavored gelatin (jelly powder), applesauce and walnuts. Cook 4 peeled and cored pears in 1/4 cup (60 mL) water in small saucepan until soft. Purée in blender. Combine cornstarch, sugar and water in medium saucepan. Add pears to saucepan. Add 1 package (3 oz., 85 g) of white grape-flavored gelatin (jelly powder). Heat and stir until sugar and gelatin are dissolved. Stir in 1/2 cup (125 mL) pecans. Pour into greased foil-lined 9 x 9 inch (22 x 22 cm) pan. Proceed as above.

GREEN APPLETS: Omit lemon-flavored gelatin (jelly powder) and walnuts. Add 1 package (3 oz., 85 g) of green apple-flavored gelatin (jelly powder). Proceed as above, using greased foil-lined 8 x 8 inch (20 x 20 cm) pan.

Two-Layer Blocks

Creamy taste and fruity goodness.

Envelopes of unflavored gelatin	4	4
(1/4 oz., 7 g, each)		
Cold water	1 cup	250 mL
Apple juice	1 1/2 cups	375 mL
Packages of strawberry-flavored gelatin	2	2
(3 oz., 85 g, each)		
Whipping cream	1 cup	250 mL

Stir unflavored gelatin into cold water in small bowl. Let stand for 10 minutes.

Bring apple juice to a boil in large saucepan. Remove from heat. Stir in flavored gelatin until dissolved. Stir in unflavored gelatin until dissolved. Return to heat. Stir in whipping cream. Pour into lightly greased 9 x 9 inch (22 x 22 cm) pan. Chill until firmly set. Sets into 2 layers. Makes 64 squares.

1 square: 26 Calories; 1.3 g Total Fat; 10 mg Sodium; 1 g Protein; 3 g Carbohydrate; trace Dietary Fiber

 To cut perfect squares, cut in half. Cut each half in half again in same direction. Cut each half in half again to make 8 rows. Repeat crosswise to make another 8 rows.

Chunky Pink Applesauce

Does double duty as a dessert with
a topping or a condiment with pork chops.

Peeled, cored cooking apples (such as Spartan or McIntosh), about 6 medium, sliced	6 cups	1.5 L
Water	2 tbsp.	30 mL
Hot cinnamon candies	1/4 cup	60 mL
Brown sugar, packed	2 tbsp.	30 mL

Place apples in 2 quart (2 L) casserole. Add water. Scatter cinnamon candies and brown sugar over apples. Cover with lid or foil. Bake in 350°F (175°C) oven for about 45 minutes. Remove cover. Bake for 10 minutes until tender and starting to break up. Chill. Makes 3 cups (750 mL).

1/2 cup (125 mL): 125 Calories; 0.4 g Total Fat; 5 mg Sodium; trace Protein; 32 g Carbohydrate; 2 g Dietary Fiber

Candied Apples

Your kids will feel like they are at the local fair.

Granulated sugar	2 cups	500 mL
White corn syrup	3/4 cup	175 mL
Boiling water	3/4 cup	175 mL
Package of cherry (or other) flavored gelatin (jelly powder)	3 oz.	85 g
Popsicle sticks	6	6
Cleaned, polished small apples, blossom and stem removed	6	6

Stir sugar, corn syrup and boiling water together in large heavy saucepan. Heat and stir until boiling and sugar is dissolved. Boil for about 20 minutes until hard crack stage (separates into hard, brittle threads) or 300°F (150°C) on candy thermometer. Turn off heat.

(continued on next page)

Snacks & Treats

Stir in gelatin until dissolved.

Insert popsicle stick into center of apple at stem end. Dip apple into gelatin mixture, tipping saucepan and swirling apple until coated. Let drip or scrap off excess along edge of saucepan. Place, stick up, on greased cookie sheet. Repeat with remaining apples. Makes 6 candied apples.

1 candied apple: 514 Calories; 0.4 g Total Fat; 71 mg Sodium; 2 g Protein; 132 g Carbohydrate; 2 g Dietary Fiber

Caramel Apples

These can be decorated while the caramel is still warm with little candies to make faces or designs.

Caramels (about 60), unwrapped	1 lb.	454 g
Milk	1 tbsp.	15 mL
Miniature marshmallows	1 cup	250 mL
Popsicle sticks	6	6
Clean, polished small apples, blossom and stem removed	6	6

Heat caramels and milk over simmering water in double boiler (see Tip) until caramels are almost melted. Stir in marshmallows. Heat and stir until smooth.

Insert popsicle stick into center of apple at stem end. Dip apple into caramel mixture, tipping saucepan and swirling apple until coated. Let drip or scrape off excess along edge of saucepan. Place, stick up, on greased cookie sheet until hardened. Repeat with remaining apples, warming caramel mixture over simmering water until desired consistency. Makes 6 caramel apples.

1 caramel apple: 394 Calories; 8.1 g Total Fat; 207 mg Sodium; 3 g Protein; 81 g Carbohydrate; 2 g Dietary Fiber

 If a recipe calls for a double boiler and you don't have one, improvise! Bring water to a simmer in small saucepan. Place a heat-proof bowl onto saucepan and you have a make-shift double boiler.

Chilled Fruit Candy

Cut these into small bite-size squares for a nutritious treat. Store in refrigerator. Squares will hold their shape for up to 2 hours at room temperature.

Package of orange-flavored gelatin (jelly powder)	3 oz.	85 g
Package of peach-flavored gelatin (jelly powder)	3 oz.	85 g
Envelopes of unflavored gelatin (1/4 oz., 7 g, each)	2	2
Boiling water	1 1/2 cups	375 mL
Can of sweetened condensed milk	11 oz.	300 mL
Finely chopped dried apricots	1/2 cup	125 mL
Finely chopped dried peaches	1/2 cup	125 mL
Chopped dried cherries	1/2 cup	125 mL

Line 9 x 13 inch (22 x 33 cm) pan with plastic wrap or aluminum foil. Mix flavored gelatins and unflavored gelatin in large bowl. Stir in boiling water until gelatin is dissolved. Stir in condensed milk. Chill for 20 minutes, stirring twice. Stir in apricots, peaches and cherries. Turn out into pan. Spread evenly. Lightly pat down. Chill for several hours until firm. Cuts into 96 squares.

1 square: 25 Calories; 0.4 g Total Fat; 10 mg Sodium; 1 g Protein; 5 g Carbohydrate; trace Dietary Fiber

Cinnamon Flatbread

A twist on the usual cinnamon toast.

Warm water	3/4 cup	175 mL
Granulated sugar	1 tsp.	5 mL
Active dry yeast	1 tsp.	5 mL
Whole wheat flour	1 1/2 cups	375 mL
Salt	1/2 tsp.	2 mL
Hard margarine (or butter), softened	1 1/2 tbsp.	25 mL
Granulated sugar	1 tbsp.	15 mL
Ground cinnamon	1/2 tsp.	2 mL

(continued on next page)

Place warm water in medium bowl. Stir in sugar until dissolved. Sprinkle yeast over water. Let stand for 10 minutes. Stir.

Add flour and salt. Stir until flour is just moistened. Turn out onto lightly floured surface. Knead until smooth. Cover. Let stand in oven with light on and door closed for 1 hour. Turn out onto lightly floured surface. Roll out into 10 inch (25 cm) circle. Place on greased baking sheet or pizza pan.

Spread margarine on dough. Combine sugar and cinnamon in small cup. Sprinkle over margarine. Firmly press fingers into dough all over surface. Bake on center rack in 400°F (205°C) oven for 15 minutes until golden. Cuts into 8 wedges.

1 wedge: 112 Calories; 2.9 g Total Fat; 200 mg Sodium; 3 g Protein; 20 g Carbohydrate; 3 g Dietary Fiber

Buttercrunch Brownies

Chocolate brownie with a chocolate bar—yummy!

Granulated sugar	1 cup	250 mL
Large eggs	2	2
Vanilla	1 tsp.	5 mL
Salt	1/4 tsp.	1 mL
Hard margarine (or butter)	1/2 cup	125 mL
Cocoa	1/3 cup	75 mL
All-purpose flour	1 1/4 cups	300 mL
Chocolate-covered crispy toffee bars (such as Heath or Skor), 1 1/2 oz. (39 g), each	4	4

Beat sugar, eggs, vanilla and salt together in medium bowl.

Melt margarine in small saucepan. Stir in cocoa. Slowly beat into egg mixture until blended. Gradually beat in flour.

Coarsely chop 3 bars. Add to ⸺ ⸺tir. Pour into well greased foil-lined 9 x 9 inch (22 x 22 ⸺⸺ ⸺nly. Finely chop remaining bar. ⸺ in 350°F (175°C) oven for about ⸺quares.

⸺ Protein; 13 g Carbohydrate;

Butterscotch Puffed Wheat Squares

A chocolaty ribbon runs through the middle of this treat.

FIRST LAYER

Hard margarine (or butter)	1/4 cup	60 mL
Butterscotch chips	3/4 cup	175 mL
Miniature marshmallows	2 1/2 cups	625 mL
Puffed wheat cereal	6 cups	1.5 L

SECOND LAYER

Hard margarine (or butter)	1/4 cup	60 mL
Semisweet chocolate chips	3/4 cup	175 mL

THIRD LAYER

Hard margarine (or butter)	1/4 cup	60 mL
Butterscotch chips	3/4 cup	175 mL
Miniature marshmallows	2 1/2 cups	625 mL
Puffed wheat cereal	6 cups	1.5 L

First Layer: Melt margarine and butterscotch chips in large saucepan. Add marshmallows. Stir until melted. Add cereal. Stir. Coat well. Pack into foil-lined 9 × 13 inch (22 × 33 cm) pan.

Second Layer: Melt margarine and chocolate chips in small saucepan. Pour and spread evenly over cereal layer.

Third Layer: Melt margarine and butterscotch chips in same large saucepan. Add marshmallows. Stir until melted. Add cereal. Stir. Coat well. Spread on chocolate chip layer. Pack down firmly. Cool at room temperature. Cuts into 32 squares.

1 square: 128 Calories; 6.1 g Total Fat; 65 mg Sodium; 1 g Protein; 18 g Carbohydrate; trace Dietary Fiber

Pictured on page 107.

Cinnamon Toasts

Suitable for a classroom snack dunked in milk.

French Vanilla cake mix (2 layer size)	1	1
Cooking oil	3/4 cup	175 mL
Large eggs	5	5
Ground cinnamon	1 tsp.	5 mL
Icing (confectioner's) sugar	2 tbsp.	30 mL

Beat cake mix, cooking oil, eggs and cinnamon in large bowl on low until moistened. Beat on high for 3 minutes. Grease and flour 11 × 17 inch (28 × 43 cm) baking sheet. Turn out batter onto sheet. Spread evenly. Bake in 325°F (160°C) oven for 30 minutes until golden brown. Let stand for 5 minutes. Cut widthwise into 4 pieces. Cut lengthwise into 8 rows. Place individual pieces 2 inches (5 cm) apart on ungreased baking sheet. Bake, in batches, in 350°F (175°C) oven for 15 minutes until cut sides are toasted and dry. Immediately remove to rack to cool for 10 minutes.

Sprinkle toasts with sieved icing sugar. Makes 32 cinnamon toasts.

1 cinnamon toast: 131 Calories; 8.1 g Total Fat; 69 mg Sodium; 2 g Protein; 13 g Carbohydrate; trace Dietary fiber

Variation: Omit French Vanilla cake mix. Use Vanilla cake mix (18 oz., 510 g). Add candy sprinkles to batter.

Variation: Omit French Vanilla cake mix. Use Chocolate Spice With Raisins cake mix.

Paré Pointer
All-star games should be held in a planetarium.

Frosty Pops

Your kids will never want any ordinary popsicle again.

Boiling water	3 cups	750 mL
Package of strawberry (or other) flavored gelatin (jelly powder)	3 oz.	85 g
Miniature marshmallows	4 cups	1 L
Paper cups (5 oz., 142 mL, each)	10	10
Popsicle sticks	10	10

Combine boiling water and gelatin in large bowl until dissolved. Chill for about 1 1/2 hours until partially set. Stir in marshmallows. Pack into cups. Insert popsicle stick into center. Freeze overnight. Makes 10 pops.

1 pop: 94 Calories; 0 g Total Fat; 41 mg Sodium; 1 g Protein; 23 g Carbohydrate; 0 g Dietary Fiber

Craft Night

1. Kids' Punch, page 149
2. Colored Popcorn, page 113
3. Paint-Box Cookies, page 92
4. Saucy Chicken Melts, page 57

Props Courtesy Of: X/S Wares

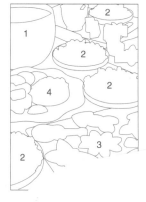

Butterscotch Toast

A sweet treat.

Brown sugar, packed	1/4 cup	60 mL
Ground cinnamon	1/2 tsp.	2 mL
Hard margarine (or butter), softened	1/4 cup	60 mL
Vanilla	1/4 tsp.	1 mL
White (or whole wheat) bread slices, crusts removed	5	5

Combine brown sugar and cinnamon in small bowl. Add margarine and vanilla. Stir until well combined.

Place bread slices on baking sheet. Broil 1 side for about 1 minute until toasted. Turn slices over. Divide and spread sugar mixture on untoasted side. Cut into 4 pieces. Broil until bubbly. Makes 20 pieces.

1 piece: 50 Calories; 2.7 g Total Fat; 62 mg Sodium; 1 g Protein; 6 g Carbohydrate; trace Dietary Fiber

Christmas Break

1. Red Hot Toddy, page 147
2. Turkey Rigatoni, page 58
3. All-Purpose Shortbread, page 87
4. Christmas Ribbons, page 141

Props Courtesy Of: Stokes
                     Winners Stores

Honey Yogurt Dip

Serve with Plain Good Chicken Fingers, page 29, or Chip 'N' Chicken Strips, page 31. For a sweet treat, surround with assorted fruit for dipping.

Plain yogurt	1 cup	250 mL
Liquid honey	1/4 cup	60 mL
Prepared mustard	2 tsp.	30 mL

Whisk all 3 ingredients in small bowl until smooth. Makes 1 1/4 cups (300 mL).

2 tbsp. (30 mL): 42 Calories; 0.4 g Total Fat; 32 mg Sodium; 1 g Protein; 9 g Carbohydrate; trace Dietary Fiber

Pictured on page 90.

Cranberry Dip

Serve with Plain Good Chicken Fingers, page 29, or Chip 'N' Chicken Strips, page 31.

Can of cranberry jelly (not whole berry sauce)	14 oz.	398 mL
Liquid honey	2 tbsp.	30 mL
Soy sauce	2 tbsp.	30 mL
Lemon juice	2 tsp.	10 mL
Cornstarch	1 tbsp.	15 mL
Freshly squeezed orange juice (about 1 medium)	1/4 cup	60 mL
Grated orange peel	1 tsp.	5 mL

Heat cranberry jelly, honey, soy sauce and lemon juice in small saucepan, stirring frequently, until starting to simmer.

Combine cornstarch and orange juice in small dish until smooth. Stir into saucepan. Simmer until thickened. Stir in orange peel. Makes 1 3/4 cups (425 mL).

2 tbsp. (30 mL): 64 Calories; 0.1 g Total Fat; 153 mg Sodium; trace Protein; 16 g Carbohydrate; trace Dietary Fiber

Chocolate Dip

Kids love to dip bananas, strawberries and plain cookies into this.

Hard margarine (or butter)	1/4 cup	60 mL
Granulated sugar	3/4 cup	175 mL
Cocoa	6 tbsp.	100 mL
Evaporated milk	1/2 cup	125 mL
Vanilla	1 tsp.	5 mL

Ground cinnamon, sprinkle

Melt margarine in small saucepan on medium-low. Stir in sugar and cocoa until well mixed. Gradually stir in evaporated milk and vanilla. Heat and stir until smooth and sugar is dissolved. Chill until thickened.

Sprinkle with cinnamon. Makes 1 1/4 cups (300 mL).

2 tbsp. (30 mL): 118 Calories; 5 g Total Fat; 71 mg Sodium; 2 g Protein; 19 g Carbohydrate; 2 g Dietary Fiber

Pictured on page 90.

Baked Salsa Cheese Dip

A big hit among teens. Serve with crunchy vegetables and nacho chips.

Light cream cheese, softened	8 oz.	250 g
Favorite Salsa, page 130 (or commercial)	1 1/3 cups	325 mL
Grated Havarti (or Monterey Jack With Jalapeño) cheese	2 cups	500 mL
Fresh cilantro, for garnish		

Combine cream cheese and salsa in medium bowl. Stir in Havarti cheese. Turn into shallow ungreased 2 quart (2 L) casserole. Cover. Bake in 325°F (160°C) oven for 45 minutes until cheese is melted and bubbling. Stir. Garnish with cilantro. Makes 3 1/3 cups (825 mL).

2 tbsp. (30 mL): 57 Calories; 4.1 g Total Fat; 318 mg Sodium; 3 g Protein; 2 g Carbohydrate; trace Dietary Fiber

Pictured on page 72.

Favorite Salsa

Make lots and store in the freezer when zucchini is plentiful.
Good with Pizza Buns, page 33, Sombreros, page 105,
and, of course, your favorite tortilla chips.

Diced zucchini, with peel	5 cups	1.25 L
Chopped onion	1 1/2 cups	375 mL
Green peppers, diced	3	3
Jalapeño peppers, finely diced (optional), see Note	4	4
Coarse pickling salt	3 tbsp.	50 mL
Cans of diced tomatoes, with juice (28 oz., 796 mL, each)	3	3
Cans of crushed tomatoes (14 oz., 398 mL, each)	2	2
Garlic clove, minced	1	1
White vinegar	3/4 cup	175 mL
Dry mustard	1 tsp.	5 mL
Salt	1/2 tsp.	2 mL
Ground cumin	1/2 tsp.	2 mL
Turmeric	1/2 tsp.	2 mL
Ground nutmeg	1/4 tsp.	1 mL
Pepper	1/4 tsp.	1 mL
Brown sugar, packed	1/2 cup	125 mL
Cornstarch	1 tbsp.	15 mL

Combine first 5 ingredients in large glass bowl. Cover. Let stand at room temperature for at least 8 hours and no longer than 24 hours. Rinse under cold running water. Drain. Repeat rinsing several times. Place in large uncovered pot or Dutch oven.

Stir in next 10 ingredients until well mixed.

Combine brown sugar and cornstarch in small bowl. Add to vegetable mixture. Stir well. Heat on medium, stirring frequently to prevent scorching, until boiling. Reduce heat to low. Simmer for 30 minutes, stirring occasionally, until vegetables are tender. Cool to room temperature. Makes 18 cups (4.5 L).

(continued on next page)

1/4 cup (60 mL): 18 Calories; 0.1 g Total Fat; 360 mg Sodium; 1 g Protein; 4 g Carbohydrate; 1 g Dietary Fiber

Pictured on page 108.

Note: Use rubber gloves when handling jalapeño peppers. Do not touch your eyes.

Chocolate Fudge

Easy to make and everyone loves it! Store in the refrigerator.

Evaporated milk	1 cup	250 mL
Granulated sugar	2 cups	500 mL
Salt	3/4 tsp.	4 mL
Miniature marshmallows	2 cups	500 mL
Semisweet chocolate chips	2 cups	500 mL
Vanilla	1 tsp.	5 mL
Chopped pecans (or walnuts), toasted (optional)	1/2 cup	125 mL

Combine evaporated milk, sugar and salt in large saucepan. Bring to a boil on medium, stirring frequently. Boil for 5 minutes without stirring. Remove from heat.

Stir in marshmallows, chocolate chips and vanilla until smooth. Stir in pecans. Pour into greased 9 × 9 inch (22 × 22 cm) pan. Cool to room temperature. Chill before cutting. Makes 2 lbs. (900 g). Cuts into 81 squares.

1 square: 50 Calories; 1.5 g Total Fat; 38 mg Sodium; 1 g Protein; 9 g Carbohydrate; trace Dietary Fiber

Pictured on page 72.

Variation: Change the chocolate chips to any flavored chips.

 To remove chocolate stains, soak the material in cold water. Spray with laundry pretreater and work in. Rinse and repeat until stain is gone. Launder.

Traffic Lights

Red light! Green light! All gone!

Hard margarine (or butter), softened	1/2 cup	125 mL
Can of sweetened condensed milk	11 oz.	300 mL
Large egg, fork-beaten	1	1
Lemon (or vanilla or almond) flavoring	1 1/2 tsp.	7 mL
All-purpose flour	2 cups	500 mL
Baking powder	2 tsp.	10 mL
Salt	1/4 tsp.	1 mL
Clear hard candies (such as Jolly Rancher), red, green and yellow (1/4 cup, 60 mL, each color)	3/4 cup	175 mL

Beat margarine, condensed milk, egg and flavoring in large bowl.

Stir in flour, baking powder and salt. Divide into 2 portions. Wrap individually with plastic wrap. Chill for at least 2 hours. Remove plastic. Knead both portions on lightly floured surface until smooth. Roll out 1 portion into 12 x 14 inch (30 x 35 cm) rectangle, 1/8 inch (3 mm) thick. Use ruler to trim edges. Cut into 2 x 4 inch (5 x 10 cm) rectangles. Cut 3 holes with floured doughnut hole cutter about 1 inch (2.5 cm) wide to resemble traffic lights. Place on greased foil-lined baking sheet. Repeat with remaining portion.

Place candies in separate plastic bags. Crush with rolling pin. Fill each hole in cookies with 1/4 tsp. (1 mL) crushed candies, one of each color. Bake on center rack in 350°F (175°C) oven for 6 to 8 minutes. Cookies may still be white or just very slightly browned on edges. Candies should be melted like glass. Let cool on pan for about 10 minutes before removing to rack to cool completely. Makes 4 dozen cookies.

1 cookie: 68 Calories; 2.9 g Total Fat; 50 mg Sodium; 1 g Protein; 9 g Carbohydrate; trace Dietary Fiber

Pictured on page 107.

Variation: Use different cookie cutters and a variety of other colors of candies to make more cookies.

Jelly Eyeballs

Perfect for that Halloween party because they are
scary looking and can be at room temperature for up to 4 hours.

Envelope of unflavored gelatin	1/4 oz.	7 g
Cold water	1/4 cup	60 mL
Boiling water	3/4 cup	175 mL
Package of cherry (or lime) flavored gelatin (jelly powder)	3 oz.	85 g
Green or red grapes, same amount as lichee fruit	17 - 20	17 - 20
Can of lichee fruit, drained	10 oz.	284 mL

Empty unflavored gelatin into medium bowl. Stir in cold water. Let stand for 5 minutes until softened. Stir in boiling water and flavored gelatin until dissolved. Chill for 50 minutes, stirring twice.

Insert grape into lichee fruit where seed has been removed. Spoon 1 tsp. (5 mL) gelatin mixture into individual lightly greased mini-muffin cups. Add 1 stuffed lichee fruit to each cup. Spoon remaining gelatin mixture over top. Chill until set. Remove with thin spatula by gently pulling gelatin away from sides of muffin pan. Chill. Makes 17 eyeballs.

1 eyeball: 30 Calories; 0.1 g Total Fat; 15 mg Sodium; 1 g Protein; 7 g Carbohydrate; trace Dietary Fiber

Pictured on page 143.

Pictured on page 143.

Paré Pointer
The first time the karate expert saluted, he cracked his helmet.

Dirt Cups

Mini cups with a creamy filling and a worm!

COOKIE CUPS		
Hard margarine (or butter), softened	1/4 cup	60 mL
Granulated sugar	1/2 cup	125 mL
Vanilla	1/4 tsp.	1 mL
Large egg	1	1
All-purpose flour	1 cup	250 mL
Cocoa	3 tbsp.	50 mL
Salt	1/8 tsp.	0.5 mL
FILLING		
Instant chocolate pudding powder (4 serving size)	1	1
Light sour cream	1/2 cup	125 mL
Cold milk	1 cup	250 mL
Chocolate cookie crumbs	1/2 cup	125 mL
Gummy worms	24	24

Cookie Cups: Cream margarine and sugar until light and fluffy. Mix in vanilla and egg until well combined. Stir in flour, cocoa and salt until dough forms a soft ball. Divide into 24 portions. Roll into balls. Press individual balls into bottom and up sides of greased mini-muffin cups. Bake in 350°F (175°C) oven for 8 to 10 minutes until firm and set. Cool. Run point of sharp knife around top edge. Remove from pans.

Filling: Beat pudding powder, sour cream and cold milk together in medium bowl for about 1 minute until smooth. Pipe into dough cups.

Sprinkle about 1 tsp. (5 mL) cookie crumbs over each pudding. Insert worm part way into filling. Makes 24 dirt cups.

1 dirt cup: 123 Calories; 3.8 g Total Fat; 177 mg Sodium; 2 g Protein; 21 g Carbohydrate; 1 g Dietary Fiber

Pictured on page 35 and back cover.

Almond Finger Cookies

Easy to shape and so delightful to eat!

Vegetable shortening (or lard), softened	1 cup	250 mL
Granulated sugar	1 cup	250 mL
Large egg	1	1
Almond flavoring	2 tsp.	10 mL
All-purpose flour, approximately	3 cups	750 mL
Baking powder	1 1/2 tsp.	7 mL
Salt	1/4 tsp.	1 mL
Ground blanched almonds	3/4 cup	175 mL
Whole blanched almonds, for nails	48 - 50	48 - 50

Beat shortening and sugar together in large bowl until light and fluffy. Beat in egg and almond flavoring.

Combine flour, baking powder and salt in medium bowl. Stir 1 cup (250 mL) flour mixture and ground almonds into shortening mixture. Gradually mix in enough remaining flour mixture until dough forms a stiff ball. Turn out onto lightly floured surface. Knead gently several times until smooth. Roll out 1/2 of dough to 1/4 inch (6 mm) thickness. Form into fingers by making ropes about 3 inches (7.5 cm) long. Squeeze with fingers to form knuckles.

Press whole almond onto end to form nail. Repeat with remaining 1/2 of dough. Bake in 350°F (175°C) oven for 10 to 13 minutes. Makes about 48 cookies.

1 cookie: 100 Calories; 6 g Total Fat; 16 mg Sodium; 1 g Protein; 10 g Carbohydrate; trace Dietary Fiber

Pictured on page 143.

WITCH'S FINGERS: Add green food coloring to the dough while kneading. For colored nails, soak whole blanched almonds in 1/4 cup (60 mL) water and 1/8 tsp. (0.5 mL) red or green food coloring for 30 minutes. Use red glossy decorating gel for cuticles.

Paré Pointer
She knew it was a baby snake because it had a rattle.

Candied Twists

Can be served as Fried Brains at your next Halloween party.

Package of popcorn twists (about 12 cups, 3 L)	6 oz.	175 g
Hard margarine (or butter)	1/2 cup	125 mL
Brown sugar, packed	1 cup	250 mL
Corn syrup	1/4 cup	60 mL
Baking soda	1/2 tsp.	2 mL
Vanilla	1 tsp.	5 mL

Place popcorn twists in large bowl.

Melt margarine in medium saucepan. Stir in brown sugar and corn syrup. Heat and stir on medium until boiling and sugar is dissolved. Boil for 2 minutes. Remove from heat.

Stir in baking soda and vanilla. Mixture will foam. Quickly pour over popcorn twists, tossing to coat well. Scrape onto greased 11 × 17 inch (28 × 43 cm) baking sheet. Bake in 250°F (120°C) oven for 30 minutes, stirring every 10 minutes. Turn out onto waxed paper to cool. Break apart several times while cooling. Makes 11 cups (2.75 L).

1 cup (250 mL): 255 Calories; 12.4 g Total Fat; 487 mg Sodium; 2 g Protein; 36 g Carbohydrate; 1 g Dietary Fiber

Pictured on page 72.

Bloody Carrot Fingers

Gruesome-looking, but good to eat.

Peeled baby carrots	20	20
Oval-shaped sliced almonds	20	20
Ketchup	2 tbsp.	30 mL

(continued on next page)

Funny Food

Cut 1/16 inch (1.5 mm) wide and 3/4 inch (2 cm) long slit into narrow end of carrot. Cut down into slit about 1/2 inch (12 mm) from end to make nail bed. Dip 1 end of almond slice into ketchup. Insert dipped end into slit. Repeat until remaining almonds are secured. Makes 20 fingers.

1 finger: 9 Calories; 0.3 g Total Fat; 23 mg Sodium; trace Protein; 1 g Carbohydrate; trace Dietary Fiber

Spiderwebs

Spiderweb filigrees of chocolate will please the partygoers!

Semisweet chocolate baking squares (1 oz., 28 g, each), cut up	3	3
Jelly bean candies		

Melt chocolate in small saucepan over hot water, or on low, stirring constantly, until smooth. Pipe in spiral design, about 4 inches (10 cm) in diameter, on waxed paper. Quickly drag point of knife through lines towards center and away from center, alternating rows. Chocolate may have to be warmed several times to maintain desired drizzling consistency. Let stand until dry and firm. Peel from waxed paper.

Place jelly bean in center of each spiderweb. Makes 8 spiderwebs.

1 spiderweb: 47 Calories; 3.3 g Total Fat; 1 mg Sodium; trace Protein; 5 g Carbohydrate; 1 g Dietary Fiber

Pictured on page 143.

BUGS: You will need 16 jelly bean candies. Cover rolling pin with waxed paper. Dab dot of chocolate onto waxed paper for body of bug. Squeeze on lines for legs (flies have 6; spiders have 8). Place 2 jelly beans in center. Let stand until dry and firm. Carefully slide waxed paper off rolling pin. Peel away. Makes 8 bugs.

Pictured on page 143.

Paré Pointer
You can make antifreeze. Just hide her blanket.

Mud Monsters

A really neat-looking cookie that adapts well for a Halloween party.

COOKIES

Hard margarine (or butter), softened	1/2 cup	125 mL
Granulated sugar	1 cup	250 mL
Cocoa	1/2 cup	125 mL
Large eggs	2	2
Vanilla	1 tsp.	5 mL
All-purpose flour	2 cups	500 mL
Baking soda	1 1/2 tsp.	7 mL
Baking powder	1/2 tsp.	2 mL
Salt	1/2 tsp.	2 mL
Milk	1 cup	250 mL

FILLING

Envelopes of dessert topping (not prepared)	2	2
Instant chocolate pudding powder (4 serving size)	1	1
Cold milk	1 1/2 cups	375 mL

Assorted candies

Cookies: Cream margarine and sugar in large bowl. Stir in cocoa until combined. Add eggs and vanilla. Mix well.

Combine flour, baking soda, baking powder and salt in medium bowl. Add to chocolate mixture, alternately with milk, beginning and ending with flour mixture. Drop 3 tbsp. (50 mL) onto greased baking sheet, about 4 inches (10 cm) apart. Bake in 425°F (220°C) oven for 10 to 11 minutes until puffy and firm. Do not overcook. Cool.

Filling: Combine dessert topping, pudding powder and cold milk in large bowl. Beat until fluffy spreading consistency. Makes 2 2/3 cup (650 mL) filling. Cut cookies into 2 layers. Spoon 2 to 3 tbsp. (30 to 50 mL) filling onto bottom half. Lay top half on top. Repeat with remaining cookies and filling.

(continued on next page)

Decorate with candies on filling to make faces. Makes 24 cookies.

1 cookie: 187 Calories; 9.2 g Total Fat; 203 mg Sodium; 3 g Protein; 25 g Carbohydrate; 1 g Dietary Fiber

Pictured on page 144.

HALLOWEEN BLACK MOONS: Omit chocolate pudding. Use same size vanilla pudding. Add enough orange food coloring to filling to make a vibrant orange.

Wormy Ice Ring

This can be put in any fruit-type punch or even just a punch bowl filled with a flavored drink mix and lemon-lime soda.

Distilled water	4 cups	1 L
Envelope of unsweetened lemon-flavored drink mix	1/4 oz.	7 g
White corn syrup	1/2 cup	125 mL
Gummy worms	20 - 22	20 - 22

Stir water, drink mix and corn syrup in 2 quart (2 L) pitcher until dissolved. Pour 1 cup (250 mL) water mixture into 6 cup (1.5 L) ring-shaped jelly mold or bundt pan. Arrange 4 to 5 worms in water mixture. Freeze until firm. Add 2 cups (500 mL) water mixture. Arrange more worms. Freeze until solid. Pour in remaining water mixture. Arrange remaining worms. Freeze until solid. To unmold, dip in warm water for an instant and turn out onto plate. Place in punch. For longer storage, freeze in resealable freezer bag. Makes 1 ice ring.

1 ice ring: 994 Calories; 1.9 g Total Fat; 169 mg Sodium; trace Protein; 14 g Carbohydrate; 0 g Dietary Fiber

WORMY ICE CUBES: Pour 1 1/2 tbsp. (25 mL) drink mixture into each ice cube tray section. Add 1 gummy worm to each section.

Rainbow Ribbons

With the many colors of flavored jelly powder, this can be made for any special occasion using appropriate colors. Be sure to check out the Halloween and Christmas variations on next page.

Packages of unflavored gelatin (1/4 oz., 7 g, each)	5	5
Cold water	1 1/4 cups	300 mL
Boiling water	5 cups	1.25 L
Package of blueberry-flavored gelatin (jelly powder)	3 oz.	85 g
Package of lemon-flavored gelatin (jelly powder)	3 oz.	85 g
Package of lime-flavored gelatin (jelly powder)	3 oz.	85 g
Package of orange-flavored gelatin (jelly powder)	3 oz.	85 g
Package of cherry-flavored gelatin (jelly powder)	3 oz.	85 g
Cold water	1/2 cup	125 mL
Packages of unflavored gelatin (1/4 oz., 7 g, each)	2	2
Boiling water	1 cup	250 mL
Can of sweetened condensed milk	11 oz.	300 mL

Lightly spray 9 x 13 inch (22 x 33 cm) pan with no-stick cooking spray. Prepare level area in refrigerator to hold pan. Pour 1 package of unflavored gelatin each into 5 separate small bowls. Stir in 1/4 cup (60 mL) cold water to each. Let stand for 5 minutes to soften. Stir in 1 cup (250 mL) boiling water and 1 package of flavored gelatin into each bowl until dissolved. Pour blueberry gelatin into pan. Chill for about 15 minutes until set.

Stir remaining cold water and remaining unflavored gelatin in medium bowl. Let stand for 5 minutes to soften. Stir in remaining boiling water and condensed milk until combined. Carefully pour 2/3 cup (150 mL) milk mixture over back of spoon onto gelatin layer. Chill for about 15 minutes. Carefully pour lemon gelatin over back of spoon onto milk layer. Chill for about 10 minutes. Alternate gelatin and 2/3 cup (150 mL) milk mixture, chilling in between for shorter and shorter periods of time, ending with cherry-flavored gelatin. Do not allow to set for too long as layers may not stick together properly. Chill, uncovered, for several hours or overnight until set. Cut with sharp knife into 1 1/2 inch (3.8 cm) squares or diamond shapes, or use cookie cutters. Makes about 48 squares.

(continued on next page)

Funny Food

Pictured on page 107.

CHRISTMAS RIBBONS: Alternate 3 red-flavored and 2 green-flavored gelatin (jelly powders) with milk layers.

Pictured on page 126.

HALLOWEEN RIBBONS: Alternate 3 black raspberry-flavored and 2 orange-flavored gelatin (jelly powders) with milk layers.

Pictured on page 143.

Egg Nests

These are always a favorite with young children.

Semisweet chocolate chips	1 cup	250 mL
Butterscotch (or peanut butter) chips	1 cup	250 mL
Steam-fried Chinese noodles	3 cups	750 mL
Small jelly bean candies	50	50

Heat and stir chocolate chips and butterscotch chips in small saucepan on low until melted.

Pour over noodles in large bowl. Stir until coated. Cluster about 1/3 cup (75 mL) on waxed paper. Make depression in center to form nest. Let stand until hardened. Chill.

Place about 5 jelly beans in each nest. Makes 10 nests.

1 nest: 227 Calories; 6.6 g Total Fat; 17 mg Sodium; 3 g Protein; 42 g Carbohydrate; 2 g Dietary Fiber

Pictured on page 53.

tip   *The ribbon dessert looks best when the darker colors are the top and bottom layers.*

Caramel Apple Drink

A very special drink!
Can easily be doubled or tripled.

Apple juice (or spiced apple drink)	1 1/4 cups	300 mL
Cinnamon stick	1	1
Frozen whipped topping	1/3 cup	75 mL
Caramel ice cream topping	1 tbsp.	15 mL

Heat juice and cinnamon stick in small saucepan until hot. Remove cinnamon stick. Pour into 12 oz. (341 mL) mug.

Top with generous swirl of whipped topping. Drizzle with caramel topping. Makes 1 drink.

1 drink: 277 Calories; 7 g Total Fat; 17 mg Sodium; 1 g Protein; 54 g Carbohydrate; trace Dietary Fiber

Halloween

1. Spiderwebs and Bugs, page 137
2. Banana Cake, page 100
3. Peanut Butter Frosting, page 101
4. Almond Finger Cookies, page 135
5. Raisin Sandwich Cookies, page 94
6. Jelly Eyeballs, page 133
7. Halloween Ribbons, page 141

Props Courtesy Of: Le Gnome
Wal-Mart Canada Inc.

Fruit Mix Shake

A thick healthy shake to enjoy as an after-school snack or for breakfast.

Sliced fresh strawberries	1 cup	250 mL
Prepared orange juice	1/4 cup	60 mL
Container of non-fat strawberry yogurt	6 oz.	175 g
Mashed bananas (about 2 small)	3/4 cup	175 mL
Liquid honey	1/2 tbsp.	7 mL
Milk (optional)		

Process first 5 ingredients in blender until smooth. Add enough milk to reach desired consistency. Serve immediately. Makes 2 cups (500 mL).

1 cup (250 mL): 188 Calories; 0.9 g Total Fat; 64 mg Sodium; 5 g Protein; 43 g Carbohydrate; 3 g Dietary Fiber

Pictured on page 89.

Sleepover

1. Tuna Pizza, page 38
2. Fruity Milk Pops, page 148
3. Mud Monsters, page 138
4. Seasoned Potato Wedges, page 79

Picnic Fruit Slush

A great take-along with a dual purpose—keeps the potato salad cold until lunch and then quenches your thirst. Don't forget to pack the soft drink.

Water	2 cups	500 mL
Granulated sugar	2 cups	500 mL
Frozen concentrated pineapple juice, thawed	12 oz.	341 mL
Ripe bananas, cut up	4	4
Large strawberries (fresh or frozen, thawed), about 9 oz., 255 g	10	10
Frozen concentrated pink lemonade	12 oz.	341 mL
Water	4 cups	1 L
Ginger ale (or lemon-lime) soft drink	4 cups	1 L

Combine first amount of water and sugar in medium saucepan. Bring to a boil. Boil for 2 minutes. Cool. Pour into 16 cup (4 L) freezer container.

Process pineapple juice concentrate and bananas in blender until smooth. Stir into water mixture.

Process strawberries and lemonade concentrate in blender until smooth. Stir into pineapple mixture. Add second amount of water. Stir. Freeze. Makes 12 cups (3 L).

Let thaw for at least 2 hours until slushy enough to spoon into glasses. Fill beverage glass 3/4 full. Add soft drink to fill. Stir. Serves 16.

1 serving: 236 Calories; 0.3 g Total Fat; 7 mg Sodium; 1 g Protein; 60 g Carbohydrate; 1 g Dietary Fiber

---

Paré Pointer

When you mix a galaxy and a toad you have star warts.

Banana Yogurt Shake

Ice creamy without the ice cream.

Milk	1 cup	250 mL
Ripe banana, cut in chunks	1	1
Container of non-fat vanilla yogurt	6 oz.	170 mL
Liquid honey	1 tbsp.	15 mL
Small ice cubes	10	10

Process first 4 ingredients in blender until smooth.

Add ice cubes, 1 at a time, through lid of blender, processing after each addition until thick and slushy. Makes 4 cups (1 L).

1 cup (250 mL): 92 Calories; 0.9 g Total Fat; 64 mg Sodium; 5 g Protein; 17 g Carbohydrate; 1 g Dietary Fiber

Pictured on page 17.

Red Hot Toddy

Kids will love the surprise at the bottom of the mug.
A real warmer-upper on a cold winter day.

Apple cider (or juice)	2 cups	500 mL
Red cinnamon heart candies	2 tbsp.	30 mL
Red cinnamon heart candies	10	10

Heat cider and first amount of candies in small saucepan on medium-high until juice is pink and candies are dissolved.

Divide second amount of candies in bottoms of 2 mugs. Divide and pour cider mixture over candies. Makes 2 cups (500 mL).

1 cup (250 mL): 205 Calories; 0 g Total Fat; 7 mg Sodium; trace Protein; 55 g Carbohydrate; 0 g Dietary Fiber

Pictured on page 126.

Orange Frost

A favorite for both ease of preparation and delicious flavor.

Prepared orange juice	1 cup	250 mL
Vanilla ice cream	2 cups	500 mL
Orange slice, cut into 3	1	1

Process orange juice and ice cream in blender until smooth. Garnish individual glasses with orange pieces. Makes 2 2/3 cups (650 mL).

1 cup (250 mL): 256 Calories; 11.4 g Total Fat; 93 mg Sodium; 4 g Protein; 35 g Carbohydrate; trace Dietary Fiber

Pictured on page 71.

Fruity Milk Pops

A variation on an old stand-by.

Packages of flavored (your choice) gelatin (jelly powder), 3 oz., 85 g, each, any flavor	2	2
Cold milk	3 cups	750 mL

Process gelatin and milk in blender for 3 minutes until frothy. Pour into plastic popsicle mold. Freeze. Makes 6 pops.

1 pop: 88 Calories; 1.5 g Total Fat; 93 mg Sodium; 11 g Protein; 13 g Carbohydrate; 0 g Dietary Fiber

Pictured on page 144.

FRUITY MILKSHAKE: Add scoop of vanilla ice cream to blender mixture. Process. Makes a filling drink.

 To keep your drink or punch from being watered down, make ice cubes from a portion of the beverage. For example, iced tea, lemonade, orange juice or cranberry cocktail, to name a few.

Melon Shake

Easy to make—so quick you could be
back on the sofa before the commercial is over!

Peeled, chopped ripe cantaloupe	1 cup	250 mL
Non-fat lemon-flavored yogurt	1 cup	250 mL
Liquid honey	2 tsp.	10 mL

Process all 3 ingredients in blender until smooth. Makes 1 1/2 cups (375 mL). Serves 1.

1 serving: 262 Calories; 1 g Total Fat; 198 mg Sodium; 13 g Protein; 54 g Carbohydrate; 1 g Dietary Fiber

Pictured on page 35 and back cover.

Kids' Punch

Ice cubes will flavor and color the soft drink.

Package of sweetened powdered drink mix, any flavor	1/4 oz.	6 g
Lemon-lime soft drink	8 cups	2 L

Prepare drink mix in 4 cup (1 L) measure as directed on package but reducing water by half. Fill ice cube trays. Freeze until solid. Makes 38 to 40 cubes.

Fill 12 cup (3 L) punch bowl 3/4 full with soft drink. Add ice cubes.

1 cup (250 mL) with 1 ice cube: 133 Calories; 0 g Total Fat; 29 mg Sodium; 0 g Protein; 34.5 g Carbohydrate; 0 g Dietary Fiber

Pictured on page 125.

Paré Pointer
You can easily tell a dogwood tree by its bark.

Snow

A perfect cooldown on a hot summer day.

Cans of pears, with juice (14 oz., 398 mL, each), cut up	2	2
Frozen concentrated apple juice, thawed	12 oz.	341 mL
Lemon-lime soft drink	4 cups	1 L
Lemon juice	2 tsp.	10 mL
Sweetened drink crystals, any flavor	1 tsp.	5 mL

Process pears with juice in blender until smooth.

Combine concentrated apple juice, soft drink and lemon juice in 10 cup (2.5 L) freezer container. Add pear purée. Freeze for 3 hours. Stir. Freeze until solid. Let stand for 10 minutes at room temperature. Scrape out with ice cream scoop. Scoop into cone-shaped paper cups or 4 oz. (114 mL) cups.

Sprinkle individual servings with 1/8 tsp. (0.5 mL) drink crystals. Makes about 8 cups (2 L).

1/2 cup (125 mL): 95 Calories; 0.1 g Total Fat; 16 mg Sodium; trace Protein; 24 g Carbohydrate; 1 g Dietary Fiber

 To reduce the cooking time for meatloaf, cook in muffin tins for half as long.

Measurement Tables

Throughout this book measurements are given in Conventional and Metric measure. To compensate for differences between the two measurements due to rounding, a full metric measure is not always used. The cup used is the standard 8 fluid ounce. Temperature is given in degrees Fahrenheit and Celsius. Baking pan measurements are in inches and centimetres as well as quarts and litres. An exact metric conversion is given below as well as the working equivalent (Standard Measure).

Spoons

Conventional Measure	Metric Exact Conversion Millilitre (mL)	Metric Standard Measure Millilitre (mL)
1/8 teaspoon (tsp.)	0.6 mL	0.5 mL
1/4 teaspoon (tsp.)	1.2 mL	1 mL
1/2 teaspoon (tsp.)	2.4 mL	2 mL
1 teaspoon (tsp.)	4.7 mL	5 mL
2 teaspoons (tsp.)	9.4 mL	10 mL
1 tablespoon (tbsp.)	14.2 mL	15 mL

Cups

Conventional Measure	Metric Exact Conversion Millilitre (mL)	Metric Standard Measure Millilitre (mL)
1/4 cup (4 tbsp.)	56.8 mL	60 mL
1/3 cup (5 1/3 tbsp.)	75.6 mL	75 mL
1/2 cup (8 tbsp.)	113.7 mL	125 mL
2/3 cup (10 2/3 tbsp.)	151.2 mL	150 mL
3/4 cup (12 tbsp.)	170.5 mL	175 mL
1 cup (16 tbsp.)	227.3 mL	250 mL
4 1/2 cups	1022.9 mL	1000 mL (1 L)

Dry Measurements

Conventional Measure Ounces (oz.)	Metric Exact Conversion Grams (g)	Metric Standard Measure Grams (g)
1 oz.	28.3 g	28 g
2 oz.	56.7 g	57 g
3 oz.	85.0 g	85 g
4 oz.	113.4 g	125 g
5 oz.	141.7 g	140 g
6 oz.	170.1 g	170 g
7 oz.	198.4 g	200 g
8 oz.	226.8 g	250 g
16 oz.	453.6 g	500 g
32 oz.	907.2 g	1000 g (1 kg)

Oven Temperatures

Fahrenheit (°F)	Celsius (°C)
175°	80°
200°	95°
225°	110°
250°	120°
275°	140°
300°	150°
325°	160°
350°	175°
375°	190°
400°	205°
425°	220°
450°	230°
475°	240°
500°	260°

Pans

Conventional Inches	Metric Centimetres
8x8 inch	20x20 cm
9x9 inch	22x22 cm
9x13 inch	22x33 cm
10x15 inch	25x38 cm
11x17 inch	28x43 cm
8x2 inch round	20x5 cm
9x2 inch round	22x5 cm
10x4 1/2 inch tube	25x11 cm
8x4x3 inch loaf	20x10x7.5 cm
9x5x3 inch loaf	22x12.5x7.5 cm

Casseroles

CANADA & BRITAIN Standard Size Casserole	Exact Metric Measure	UNITED STATES Standard Size Casserole	Exact Metric Measure
1 qt. (5 cups)	1.13 L	1 qt. (4 cups)	900 mL
1 1/2 qts. (7 1/2 cups)	1.69 L	1 1/2 qts. (6 cups)	1.35 L
2 qts. (10 cups)	2.25 L	2 qts. (8 cups)	1.8 L
2 1/2 qts. (12 1/2 cups)	2.81 L	2 1/2 qts. (10 cups)	2.25 L
3 qts. (15 cups)	3.38 L	3 qts. (12 cups)	2.7 L
4 qts. (20 cups)	4.5 L	4 qts. (16 cups)	3.6 L
5 qts. (25 cups)	5.63 L	5 qts. (20 cups)	4.5 L

Photo Index

Tip Index

Recipe Index

155

157

Company's Coming cookbooks are available at **retail locations** throughout Canada!

See mail order form

Buy any 2 cookbooks—choose a 3rd FREE of equal or less value than the lowest price paid. *Available in French

Original Series — CA$14.99 Canada — US$10.99 USA & International

CODE		CODE		CODE	
SQ	150 Delicious Squares*	BA	Barbecues*	PZ	Pizza*
CA	Casseroles*	PI	Pies*	ODM	One Dish Meals*
MU	Muffins & More*	LR	Light Recipes*	ST	Starters*
SA	Salads*	PR	Preserves*	SF	Stir-Fry*
AP	Appetizers	LCA	Light Casseroles*	MAM	Make-Ahead Meals*
DE	Desserts	CH	Chicken*	PB	The Potato Book*
SS	Soups & Sandwiches	KC	Kids Cooking	CCLFC	Low-Fat Cooking*
CO	Cookies*	BR	Breads*	CCLFP	Low-Fat Pasta*
VE	Vegetables	ME	Meatless Cooking*	AC	Appliance Cooking*
MC	Main Courses	CT	Cooking For Two*	CFK	Cook For Kids
PA	Pasta*	BB	Breakfasts & Brunches*	SCH	Stews, Chilies & Chowd•
CK	Cakes	SC	Slow Cooker Recipes*		**NEW** *Oct 1/01*

Greatest Hits — CA$12.99 Canada — US$9.99 USA & International

CODE		CODE		CODE	
BML	Biscuits, Muffins & Loaves*	SAS	Soups & Salads*	ITAL	Italian
DSD	Dips, Spreads & Dressings*	SAW	Sandwiches & Wraps*	MEX	Mexican

Lifestyle Series — CA$16.99 Canada — US$12.99 USA & International

CODE	
GR	Grilling*
DC	Diabetic Cooking*

Special Occasion Series — CA$19.99 Canada — US$19.99 USA & International

CODE	
CE	Chocolate Everything*
GFK	Gifts from the Kitchen **NEW** *Sept 1/01*

COOKBOOKS ®

www.**companys**coming.com
visit our web-site

COMPANY'S COMING PUBLISHING LIMITED
2311 - 96 Street
Edmonton, Alberta, Canada T6N 1G3
Tel: (780) 450-6223 Fax: (780) 450-1857

Exclusive Mail Order Offer

See page 158 for list of cookbooks

Buy 2 Get 1 FREE!
Buy any 2 cookbooks—choose a **3rd FREE** of equal or less value than the lowest price paid.

Quantity	Code	Title	Price Each	Price Total
			$	$
		don't forget		
		to indicate your		
		free book(s).		
		(see exclusive mail order		
		offer above)		
		please print		
	TOTAL BOOKS (including FREE)	**TOTAL BOOKS PURCHASED:**	$	

	International		Canada & USA	
Plus Shipping & Handling (per destination)	$7.00	(one book)	$5.00	(1-3 books)
Additional Books (including FREE books)	$	($2.00 each)	$	($1.00 each)
Sub-Total	$		$	
Canadian residents add G.S.T(7%)			$	
TOTAL AMOUNT ENCLOSED	$		$	

The Fine Print

- Orders outside Canada must be **PAID IN US FUNDS** by cheque or money order drawn on Canadian or US bank or by credit card.
- Make cheque or money order payable to: **COMPANY'S COMING PUBLISHING LIMITED.**
- Prices are expressed in Canadian dollars for Canada, US dollars for USA & International and are subject to change without prior notice.
- Orders are shipped surface mail. For courier rates, visit our web-site: **www.companyscoming.com** or contact us: **Tel: (780) 450-6223 Fax: (780) 450-1857.**
- Sorry, no C.O.D's.

☐ MasterCard ☐ VISA

_____
Expiry date

Account # _____

Name of cardholder _____

Cardholder's signature _____

Shipping Address
Send the cookbooks listed above to:

Name: _____

Street: _____

City: _____ Prov./State: _____

Country: _____ Postal Code/Zip: _____

Tel: ( ) _____

E-mail address: _____

YES! Please send a catalogue: ☐ English ☐ French

Gift Giving

- Let us help you with your gift giving!
- We will send cookbooks directly to the recipients of your choice if you give us their names and addresses.
- Please specify the titles you wish to send to each person.
- If you would like to include your personal note or card, we will be pleased to enclose it with your gift order.
- Company's Coming Cookbooks make excellent gifts: Birthdays, bridal showers, Mother's Day, Father's Day, graduation or any occasion...collect them all!

Please mail or fax to:
Company's Coming Publishing Limited
2311 - 96 Street
Edmonton, Alberta, Canada   T6N 1G3
Fax: (780) 450-1857

Name:_____

Address:_____

_____

e-mail:_____

Reader Survey

We welcome your comments and would love to hear from you.
Please take a few moments to give us your feedback.

1. *Approximately what percentage of the cooking do you do in your home?*_____ %

2. *How many meals do you cook in your home in a typical week?* _____

3. *How often do you refer to a cookbook (or other source) for recipes?*

❑ Everyday ❑ 2 or 3 times a month ❑ A few times a year
❑ A few times a week ❑ Once a month ❑ Never

4. *What recipe features are most important to you? Rank 1 to 7;*
(1 being most important, 7 being least important).

——— Recipes for everyday cooking
——— Recipes for guests and entertaining
——— Easy recipes; quick to prepare, with everyday ingredients
——— Low-fat or health-conscious recipes
——— Recipes you can trust to work
——— Recipes using exotic ingredients
——— Recipes using fresh ingredients only

5. *What cookbook features are most important to you? Rank 1 to 6;*
(1 being most important, 6 being least important).

_____ Lots of color photographs of recipes
_____ "How-to" instructions or photos
_____ Helpful hints & cooking tips
_____ Lay-flat binding (coil or plastic comb)
_____ Well organized with complete index
_____ Priced low

6. *How many cookbooks have you purchased in the last year?*_____

7. *Of these, how many were gifts?*_____

8. *Age group*

❑ Under 18 ❑ 25 to 34 ❑ 45 to 54 ❑ 65+
❑ 18 to 24 ❑ 35 to 44 ❑ 55 to 64

9. *What do you like best about Company's Coming Cookbooks?*

_____

_____

10. *How could Company's Coming Cookbooks be improved?*

_____

_____

11. *Topics you would like to see published by Company's Coming:*

_____

_____

Thank you for sharing your views. We truly value your input.